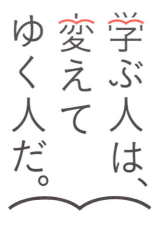

学ぶ人は、
変えて
ゆく人だ。

目の前にある問題はもちろん、

人生の問いや、

社会の課題を自ら見つけ、

挑み続けるために、人は学ぶ。

「学び」で、

少しずつ世界は変えてゆける。

いつでも、どこでも、誰でも、

学ぶことができる世の中へ。

旺文社

JN247535

2020 年度版

文部科学省後援

英検® 3級
過去6回 全問題集

旺文社

この問題カードは切り取って，本番の面接の練習用にしてください。
質問は p.37 にありますので，参考にしてください。

International Supermarkets

There are many international supermarkets in Japan. International supermarkets sell interesting food from different countries, so they are popular with many people. The food at these stores is sometimes expensive.

問題カード

この問題カードは切り取って，本番の面接の練習用にしてください。
質問は p.39 にありますので，参考にしてください。

Concerts

Watching famous singers or bands on stage is exciting. Many people enjoy going to concerts with their friends, but some people like watching concerts alone. Music festivals are often held outside in summer.

問題カード

この問題カードは切り取って，本番の面接の練習用にしてください。
質問は p.61 にありますので，参考にしてください。

A Popular Japanese Food

Tofu is used in many delicious Japanese dishes. Some people like to put it in salad, soup, and even ice cream and cake. Tofu is healthy and cheap, so it is eaten by many people.

この問題カードは切り取って，本番の面接の練習用にしてください。
質問は p.63 にありますので，参考にしてください。

Health Clubs

In Japan, there are lots of health clubs. Many people want to stay strong and healthy, so they become members of health clubs. Sometimes, people can make new friends there, too.

この問題カードは切り取って，本番の面接の練習用にしてください。
質問は p.85 にありますので，参考にしてください。

A Popular Food

Tempura is a popular Japanese food. Fresh vegetables and seafood are cooked in hot oil. Many people enjoy eating tempura at restaurants, but some people like to make tempura at home.

問題カード

この問題カードは切り取って，本番の面接の練習用にしてください。
質問は p.87 にありますので，参考にしてください。

The Winter Games

The Winter Olympic Games are an international sports event. People from many countries try hard to win a gold medal. Snowboarding and skating are exciting to watch, so they are enjoyed by many people.

2019年度第2回 英検3級 解答用紙

【注意事項】
①解答にはHBの黒鉛筆(シャープペンシルも可)を使用し，解答を訂正する場合には消しゴムで完全に消してください。
②解答用紙は絶対に汚したり折り曲げたり，所定以外のところへの記入はしないでください。

③マーク例

	良い例	悪い例
	●	◑ ✖ ◐

 これ以下の濃さのマークは読めません。

解 答 欄

問題番号	1	2	3	4
(1)	①	②	③	④
(2)	①	②	③	④
(3)	①	②	③	④
(4)	①	②	③	④
(5)	①	②	③	④
(6)	①	②	③	④
(7)	①	②	③	④
(8)	①	②	③	④
(9)	①	②	③	④
(10)	①	②	③	④
(11)	①	②	③	④
(12)	①	②	③	④
(13)	①	②	③	④
(14)	①	②	③	④
(15)	①	②	③	④

問題番号1

解 答 欄

問題番号	1	2	3	4
(16)	①	②	③	④
(17)	①	②	③	④
(18)	①	②	③	④
(19)	①	②	③	④
(20)	①	②	③	④
(21)	①	②	③	④
(22)	①	②	③	④
(23)	①	②	③	④
(24)	①	②	③	④
(25)	①	②	③	④
(26)	①	②	③	④
(27)	①	②	③	④
(28)	①	②	③	④
(29)	①	②	③	④
(30)	①	②	③	④

問題番号2 (16)〜(20)、3 (21)〜(30)

※筆記4の解答欄はこの裏にあります。

リスニング解答欄

問題番号	1	2	3	4
例題	①	②	●	
No. 1	①	②	③	
No. 2	①	②	③	
No. 3	①	②	③	
No. 4	①	②	③	
No. 5	①	②	③	
No. 6	①	②	③	
No. 7	①	②	③	
No. 8	①	②	③	
No. 9	①	②	③	
No. 10	①	②	③	
No. 11	①	②	③	④
No. 12	①	②	③	④
No. 13	①	②	③	④
No. 14	①	②	③	④
No. 15	①	②	③	④
No. 16	①	②	③	④
No. 17	①	②	③	④
No. 18	①	②	③	④
No. 19	①	②	③	④
No. 20	①	②	③	④
No. 21	①	②	③	④
No. 22	①	②	③	④
No. 23	①	②	③	④
No. 24	①	②	③	④
No. 25	①	②	③	④
No. 26	①	②	③	④
No. 27	①	②	③	④
No. 28	①	②	③	④
No. 29	①	②	③	④
No. 30	①	②	③	④

第1部 No.1〜No.10、第2部 No.11〜No.20、第3部 No.21〜No.30

2019年度第2回

Web特典「自動採点サービス」対応 オンラインマークシート

※検定の回によってQRコードが違います。
※筆記1〜3，リスニングの採点ができます。
※PCからも利用できます(問題編 p.8 参照)。

※実際の解答用紙に似せていますが，デザイン・サイズは異なります。

●記入上の注意（記述形式）
・指示事項を守り，文字は，はっきりと分かりやすく書いてください。
・太枠に囲まれた部分のみが採点の対象です。

4 ライティング解答欄

5

10

2019年度第1回　英検3級　解答用紙

【注意事項】
①解答にはHBの黒鉛筆（シャープペンシルも可）を使用し，解答を訂正する場合には消しゴムで完全に消してください。
②解答用紙は絶対に汚したり折り曲げたり，所定以外のところへの記入はしないでください。

③マーク例

良い例	悪い例
●	◑ ✖ ◓

これ以下の濃さのマークは読めません。

解　答　欄

問題番号	1	2	3	4
1 (1)	①	②	③	④
(2)	①	②	③	④
(3)	①	②	③	④
(4)	①	②	③	④
(5)	①	②	③	④
(6)	①	②	③	④
(7)	①	②	③	④
(8)	①	②	③	④
(9)	①	②	③	④
(10)	①	②	③	④
(11)	①	②	③	④
(12)	①	②	③	④
(13)	①	②	③	④
(14)	①	②	③	④
(15)	①	②	③	④

解　答　欄

問題番号	1	2	3	4
2 (16)	①	②	③	④
(17)	①	②	③	④
(18)	①	②	③	④
(19)	①	②	③	④
(20)	①	②	③	④
3 (21)	①	②	③	④
(22)	①	②	③	④
(23)	①	②	③	④
(24)	①	②	③	④
(25)	①	②	③	④
(26)	①	②	③	④
(27)	①	②	③	④
(28)	①	②	③	④
(29)	①	②	③	④
(30)	①	②	③	④

※筆記4の解答欄はこの裏にあります。

リスニング解答欄

問題番号	1	2	3	4
例題	①	②	●	
第1部 No. 1	①	②	③	
No. 2	①	②	③	
No. 3	①	②	③	
No. 4	①	②	③	
No. 5	①	②	③	
No. 6	①	②	③	
No. 7	①	②	③	
No. 8	①	②	③	
No. 9	①	②	③	
No. 10	①	②	③	
第2部 No. 11	①	②	③	④
No. 12	①	②	③	④
No. 13	①	②	③	④
No. 14	①	②	③	④
No. 15	①	②	③	④
No. 16	①	②	③	④
No. 17	①	②	③	④
No. 18	①	②	③	④
No. 19	①	②	③	④
No. 20	①	②	③	④
第3部 No. 21	①	②	③	④
No. 22	①	②	③	④
No. 23	①	②	③	④
No. 24	①	②	③	④
No. 25	①	②	③	④
No. 26	①	②	③	④
No. 27	①	②	③	④
No. 28	①	②	③	④
No. 29	①	②	③	④
No. 30	①	②	③	④

2019年度第1回

Web特典「自動採点サービス」対応 オンラインマークシート
※検定の回によってQRコードが違います。
※筆記1〜3，リスニングの採点ができます。
※PCからも利用できます（問題編 p.8 参照）。

※実際の解答用紙に似せていますが，デザイン・サイズは異なります。

●記入上の注意（記述形式）
・指示事項を守り，文字は，はっきりと分かりやすく書いてください。
・太枠に囲まれた部分のみが採点の対象です。

4 ライティング解答欄

5

10

【注意事項】

①解答にはHBの黒鉛筆(シャープペンシルも可)を使用し，解答を訂正する場合には消しゴムで完全に消してください。

②解答用紙は絶対に汚したり折り曲げたり，所定以外のところへの記入はしないでください。

③マーク例

良い例	悪い例
●	⑴ ✗ ⬗

これ以下の濃さのマークは読めません。

解　答　欄

問題番号	1	2	3	4
(1)	①	②	③	④
(2)	①	②	③	④
(3)	①	②	③	④
(4)	①	②	③	④
(5)	①	②	③	④
(6)	①	②	③	④
(7)	①	②	③	④
(8)	①	②	③	④
(9)	①	②	③	④
(10)	①	②	③	④
(11)	①	②	③	④
(12)	①	②	③	④
(13)	①	②	③	④
(14)	①	②	③	④
(15)	①	②	③	④

1

解　答　欄

問題番号	1	2	3	4
(16)	①	②	③	④
(17)	①	②	③	④
(18)	①	②	③	④
(19)	①	②	③	④
(20)	①	②	③	④
(21)	①	②	③	④
(22)	①	②	③	④
(23)	①	②	③	④
(24)	①	②	③	④
(25)	①	②	③	④
(26)	①	②	③	④
(27)	①	②	③	④
(28)	①	②	③	④
(29)	①	②	③	④
(30)	①	②	③	④

2 ((16)〜(20))
3 ((21)〜(30))

※筆記4の解答欄はこの裏にあります。

リスニング解答欄

問題番号	1	2	3	4
例題	①	②	●	
No. 1	①	②	③	
No. 2	①	②	③	
No. 3	①	②	③	
No. 4	①	②	③	
No. 5	①	②	③	
No. 6	①	②	③	
No. 7	①	②	③	
No. 8	①	②	③	
No. 9	①	②	③	
No. 10	①	②	③	
No. 11	①	②	③	④
No. 12	①	②	③	④
No. 13	①	②	③	④
No. 14	①	②	③	④
No. 15	①	②	③	④
No. 16	①	②	③	④
No. 17	①	②	③	④
No. 18	①	②	③	④
No. 19	①	②	③	④
No. 20	①	②	③	④
No. 21	①	②	③	④
No. 22	①	②	③	④
No. 23	①	②	③	④
No. 24	①	②	③	④
No. 25	①	②	③	④
No. 26	①	②	③	④
No. 27	①	②	③	④
No. 28	①	②	③	④
No. 29	①	②	③	④
No. 30	①	②	③	④

第1部 (No. 1〜No. 10)
第2部 (No. 11〜No. 20)
第3部 (No. 21〜No. 30)

2018年度第3回

Web特典「自動採点サービス」対応 オンラインマークシート

※検定の回によってQRコードが違います。
※筆記1〜3，リスニングの採点ができます。
※ PCからも利用できます (問題編 p.8 参照)。

※実際の解答用紙に似せていますが，デザイン・サイズは異なります。

左余白（縦書き）：切り取り線

●記入上の注意（記述形式）
・指示事項を守り，文字は，はっきりと分かりやすく書いてください。
・太枠に囲まれた部分のみが採点の対象です。

4 ライティング解答欄

5

10

2018年度第2回　英検3級　解答用紙

[注意事項]

①解答にはHBの黒鉛筆（シャープペンシルも可）を使用し，解答を訂正する場合には消しゴムで完全に消してください。

②解答用紙は絶対に汚したり折り曲げたり，所定以外のところへの記入はしないでください。

③マーク例

良い例	悪い例
●	◑ ✕ ◔

これ以下の濃さのマークは読めません。

解　答　欄				
問題番号	1	2	3	4
(1)	①	②	③	④
(2)	①	②	③	④
(3)	①	②	③	④
(4)	①	②	③	④
(5)	①	②	③	④
(6)	①	②	③	④
(7)	①	②	③	④
(8)	①	②	③	④
(9)	①	②	③	④
(10)	①	②	③	④
(11)	①	②	③	④
(12)	①	②	③	④
(13)	①	②	③	④
(14)	①	②	③	④
(15)	①	②	③	④

（左表の問題番号は 1）

解　答　欄				
問題番号	1	2	3	4
(16)	①	②	③	④
(17)	①	②	③	④
(18)	①	②	③	④
(19)	①	②	③	④
(20)	①	②	③	④
(21)	①	②	③	④
(22)	①	②	③	④
(23)	①	②	③	④
(24)	①	②	③	④
(25)	①	②	③	④
(26)	①	②	③	④
(27)	①	②	③	④
(28)	①	②	③	④
(29)	①	②	③	④
(30)	①	②	③	④

（(16)〜(20)は 2，(21)〜(30)は 3）

※筆記4の解答欄はこの裏にあります。

リスニング解答欄				
問題番号	1	2	3	4
例題	①	②	●	
No. 1	①	②	③	
No. 2	①	②	③	
No. 3	①	②	③	
No. 4	①	②	③	
No. 5	①	②	③	
No. 6	①	②	③	
No. 7	①	②	③	
No. 8	①	②	③	
No. 9	①	②	③	
No. 10	①	②	③	
No. 11	①	②	③	④
No. 12	①	②	③	④
No. 13	①	②	③	④
No. 14	①	②	③	④
No. 15	①	②	③	④
No. 16	①	②	③	④
No. 17	①	②	③	④
No. 18	①	②	③	④
No. 19	①	②	③	④
No. 20	①	②	③	④
No. 21	①	②	③	④
No. 22	①	②	③	④
No. 23	①	②	③	④
No. 24	①	②	③	④
No. 25	①	②	③	④
No. 26	①	②	③	④
No. 27	①	②	③	④
No. 28	①	②	③	④
No. 29	①	②	③	④
No. 30	①	②	③	④

（No.1〜No.10は 第1部，No.11〜No.20は 第2部，No.21〜No.30は 第3部）

2018年度第2回

Web特典「自動採点(さい)サービス」対応(おう) オンラインマークシート

※検定(けん)の回によってQRコードが違(ちが)います。

※筆記1〜3，リスニングの採点(さい)ができます。

※PCからも利用できます（問題編(へん) p.8 参照）。

※実際の解答用紙に似せていますが，デザイン・サイズは異なります。

●記入上の注意（記述形式）
・指示事項を守り，文字は，はっきりと分かりやすく書いてください。
・太枠に囲まれた部分のみが採点の対象です。

4 ライティング解答欄

5

10

2018年度第1回　英検3級　解答用紙

【注意事項】

①解答にはHBの黒鉛筆（シャープペンシルも可）を使用し，解答を訂正する場合には消しゴムで完全に消してください。

②解答用紙は絶対に汚したり折り曲げたり，所定以外のところへの記入はしないでください。

③マーク例

良い例	悪い例
●	◓ ✖ ◗

 これ以下の濃さのマークは読めません。

解　答　欄

問題番号	1	2	3	4
(1)	①	②	③	④
(2)	①	②	③	④
(3)	①	②	③	④
(4)	①	②	③	④
(5)	①	②	③	④
(6)	①	②	③	④
(7)	①	②	③	④
(8)	①	②	③	④
(9)	①	②	③	④
(10)	①	②	③	④
(11)	①	②	③	④
(12)	①	②	③	④
(13)	①	②	③	④
(14)	①	②	③	④
(15)	①	②	③	④

（問題番号1の欄）

解　答　欄

問題番号	1	2	3	4
(16)	①	②	③	④
(17)	①	②	③	④
(18)	①	②	③	④
(19)	①	②	③	④
(20)	①	②	③	④
(21)	①	②	③	④
(22)	①	②	③	④
(23)	①	②	③	④
(24)	①	②	③	④
(25)	①	②	③	④
(26)	①	②	③	④
(27)	①	②	③	④
(28)	①	②	③	④
(29)	①	②	③	④
(30)	①	②	③	④

（問題番号2は(16)〜(20)，3は(21)〜(30)）

※筆記4の解答欄はこの裏にあります。

リスニング解答欄

問題番号	1	2	3	4
例題	①	②	●	
No. 1	①	②	③	
No. 2	①	②	③	
No. 3	①	②	③	
No. 4	①	②	③	
No. 5	①	②	③	
No. 6	①	②	③	
No. 7	①	②	③	
No. 8	①	②	③	
No. 9	①	②	③	
No. 10	①	②	③	
No. 11	①	②	③	④
No. 12	①	②	③	④
No. 13	①	②	③	④
No. 14	①	②	③	④
No. 15	①	②	③	④
No. 16	①	②	③	④
No. 17	①	②	③	④
No. 18	①	②	③	④
No. 19	①	②	③	④
No. 20	①	②	③	④
No. 21	①	②	③	④
No. 22	①	②	③	④
No. 23	①	②	③	④
No. 24	①	②	③	④
No. 25	①	②	③	④
No. 26	①	②	③	④
No. 27	①	②	③	④
No. 28	①	②	③	④
No. 29	①	②	③	④
No. 30	①	②	③	④

（第1部 No.1〜No.10，第2部 No.11〜No.20，第3部 No.21〜No.30）

2018年度第1回

Web特典「自動採点サービス」対応
オンラインマークシート

※検定の回によってQRコードが違います。
※筆記1〜3，リスニングの採点ができます。
※PCからも利用できます（問題編 p.8 参照）。

※実際の解答用紙に似せていますが，デザイン・サイズは異なります。

●**記入上の注意（記述形式）**
・指示事項を守り，文字は，はっきりと分かりやすく書いてください。
・太枠に囲まれた部分のみが採点の対象です。

4 ライティング解答欄

5

10

2017年度第3回　英検3級　解答用紙

【注意事項】

① 解答にはHBの黒鉛筆（シャープペンシルも可）を使用し，解答を訂正する場合には消しゴムで完全に消してください。

② 解答用紙は絶対に汚したり折り曲げたり，所定以外のところへの記入はしないでください。

③ マーク例

良い例	悪い例
●	◑ ✗ ◓

これ以下の濃さのマークは読めません。

解　答　欄

問題番号	1	2	3	4
(1)	①	②	③	④
(2)	①	②	③	④
(3)	①	②	③	④
(4)	①	②	③	④
(5)	①	②	③	④
(6)	①	②	③	④
(7)	①	②	③	④
(8)	①	②	③	④
(9)	①	②	③	④
(10)	①	②	③	④
(11)	①	②	③	④
(12)	①	②	③	④
(13)	①	②	③	④
(14)	①	②	③	④
(15)	①	②	③	④

（左欄全体の問題番号：1）

解　答　欄

問題番号	1	2	3	4
(16)	①	②	③	④
(17)	①	②	③	④
(18)	①	②	③	④
(19)	①	②	③	④
(20)	①	②	③	④
(21)	①	②	③	④
(22)	①	②	③	④
(23)	①	②	③	④
(24)	①	②	③	④
(25)	①	②	③	④
(26)	①	②	③	④
(27)	①	②	③	④
(28)	①	②	③	④
(29)	①	②	③	④
(30)	①	②	③	④

（(16)〜(20)：2　(21)〜(30)：3）

※筆記4の解答欄はこの裏にあります。

リスニング解答欄

問題番号	1	2	3	4
例題	①	②	●	
No. 1	①	②	③	
No. 2	①	②	③	
No. 3	①	②	③	
No. 4	①	②	③	
No. 5	①	②	③	
No. 6	①	②	③	
No. 7	①	②	③	
No. 8	①	②	③	
No. 9	①	②	③	
No. 10	①	②	③	
No. 11	①	②	③	④
No. 12	①	②	③	④
No. 13	①	②	③	④
No. 14	①	②	③	④
No. 15	①	②	③	④
No. 16	①	②	③	④
No. 17	①	②	③	④
No. 18	①	②	③	④
No. 19	①	②	③	④
No. 20	①	②	③	④
No. 21	①	②	③	④
No. 22	①	②	③	④
No. 23	①	②	③	④
No. 24	①	②	③	④
No. 25	①	②	③	④
No. 26	①	②	③	④
No. 27	①	②	③	④
No. 28	①	②	③	④
No. 29	①	②	③	④
No. 30	①	②	③	④

（No. 1〜No. 10：第1部　No. 11〜No. 20：第2部　No. 21〜No. 30：第3部）

2017年度第3回

Web特典「自動採点サービス」対応オンラインマークシート

※検定の回によってQRコードが違います。

※筆記1〜3，リスニングの採点ができます。

※PCからも利用できます（問題編 p.8 参照）。

※実際の解答用紙に似せていますが，デザイン・サイズは異なります。

●記入上の注意（記述形式）
・指示事項を守り，文字は，はっきりと分かりやすく書いてください。
・太枠に囲まれた部分のみが採点の対象です。

4 ライティング解答欄

| |
| |
| 5 |
| |
| 10 |

Introduction

はじめに

実用英語技能検定（英検®）は，年間受験者数380万人（英検IBA，英検Jr.との総数）の小学生から社会人まで，幅広い層が受験する国内最大級の資格試験で，1963年の第1回検定からの累計では1億人を超える人々が受験しています。英検®は，コミュニケーションに欠かすことのできない4技能をバランスよく測定することを目的としており，英検®の受験によってご自身の英語力を把握できるだけでなく，進学・就職・留学などの場面で多くのチャンスを手に入れることにつながります。

この『全問題集シリーズ』は，英語を学ぶ皆さまを応援する気持ちを込めて刊行しました。本書は，2019年度第2回検定を含む6回分の過去問を，皆さまの理解が深まるよう，日本語訳や詳しい解説を加えて収録しています。

本書が皆さまの英検合格の足がかりとなり，さらには国際社会で活躍できるような生きた英語を身につけるきっかけとなることを願っています。

最後に，本書を刊行するにあたり，多大なご尽力をいただきました敬愛大学教授 向後秀明先生に深く感謝の意を表します。

2020年　春

※本書に掲載している過去問は，公益財団法人 日本英語検定協会が公表しているもののみです。準会場・海外受験などの問題とは一致しない可能性があります。
※二次試験の問題カードは日本英語検定協会から提供を受けたもののみ掲載しています。

もくじ

Contents

※本書に収録されている英検の過去問は「従来型」のものになります。なお，従来型と新方式は問題形式・内容は全く変わりません。実施方式が変わるだけです。

執　　筆：向後秀明（敬愛大学）
編集協力：株式会社 カルチャー・プロ，入江 泉
録　　音：ユニバ合同会社
デザイン：林 慎一郎（及川真咲デザイン事務所）
組版・データ作成協力：幸和印刷株式会社

本書の使い方

ここでは，本書の過去問および特典についての活用法の一例を紹介します。

本書の内容

過去問 6回分	英検 インフォ メーション (p.10-13)	2019年度の 傾向と 攻略ポイント (p.14-16)	二次試験・ 面接の流れ (p.9)	Web特典 (p.7-8)

本書の使い方

一次試験対策

情報収集・傾向把握
・英検インフォメーション
・2019年度の傾向と攻略ポイント

過去問にチャレンジ
・2019年度第2回一次試験
・2019年度第1回一次試験
・2018年度第3回一次試験
・2018年度第2回一次試験
・2018年度第1回一次試験
・2017年度第3回一次試験
※【Web特典】自動採点サービスの活用

二次試験対策

情報収集・傾向把握
・二次試験・面接の流れ
・【Web特典】
　面接シミュレーション／面接模範例

過去問にチャレンジ
・2019年度第2回二次試験
・2019年度第1回二次試験
・2018年度第3回二次試験
・2018年度第2回二次試験
・2018年度第1回二次試験
・2017年度第3回二次試験

過去問の取り組み方

1セット目

【本番モード】
本番の試験と同じように，制限時間を設けて取り組みましょう。どの問題形式に時間がかかりすぎているか，正答率が低いかなど，今のあなたの実力を把握しましょう。
「自動採点サービス」を活用して，答え合わせをスムーズに行いましょう。

2〜5セット目

【学習モード】
制限時間をなくし，解けるまで取り組みましょう。
リスニングは音声を繰り返し聞いて解答を導き出してもかまいません。すべての問題に正解できるまで見直します。

6セット目

【仕上げモード】
試験直前の仕上げに利用しましょう。時間を計って本番のつもりで取り組みます。
これまでに取り組んだ6セットの過去問で間違えた問題の解説を本番試験の前にもう一度見直しましょう。

音声について

一次試験・リスニングと二次試験・面接の音声を聞くことができます。本書とともに使い，効果的なリスニング・面接対策をしましょう。

収録内容と特長

 ### 一次試験・リスニング

| 本番の試験の音声を収録 | ➡ | スピードをつかめる！ |

※2018年度第1回，2017年度第3回については，旺文社が独自に収録し直した音声です。

| 解答時間は本番通り10秒間 | ➡ | 解答時間に慣れる！ |

| 収録されている英文は，別冊解答に掲載 | ➡ | 聞き取れない箇所を確認できる！ |

 ### 二次試験・面接（スピーキング）

| 実際の流れ通りに収録 | ➡ | 本番の雰囲気を味わえる！ |

・パッセージの黙読（試験通り20秒の黙読時間があります）
・パッセージの音読（Model Readingを収録しています）
・質問（音声を一時停止してご利用ください）

| 各質問のModel Answerも収録 | ➡ | 模範解答が確認できる！ |

| Model Answerは，別冊解答に掲載 | ➡ | 聞き取れない箇所を確認できる！ |

3つの方法で音声が聞けます！

① 公式アプリ「英語の友」（iOS/Android）で お手軽再生

リスニング力を強化する機能満載

- 再生速度変換（0.5～2.0倍速）
- お気に入り機能（絞込み学習）
- オフライン再生
- バックグラウンド再生
- 試験日カウントダウン

［ご利用方法］

1 「英語の友」公式サイトより，アプリをインストール
https://eigonotomo.com/ 　英語の友 🔍
（右のQRコードから読み込めます）

2 アプリ内のライブラリよりご購入いただいた書籍を選び，「追加」ボタンを押してください

3 パスワードを入力すると，音声がダウンロードできます
[パスワード：avtphc] ※すべて半角アルファベット小文字

※本アプリの機能の一部は有料ですが，本書の音声は無料でお聞きいただけます。
※詳しいご利用方法は「英語の友」公式サイト，あるいはアプリ内ヘルプをご参照ください。
※2020年2月20日から2021年8月31日までご利用いただけます。
※本サービスは，上記ご利用期間内でも予告なく終了することがあります。

CDをご希望の方は，別売「2020年度版英検3級過去6回全問題集CD」
（本体価格1,000円+税）をご利用ください。

持ち運びに便利な小冊子とCD3枚付き。CDプレーヤーで通して聞くと，本番と同じような環境で練習できます。　※収録箇所は，本書で **CD 1 1** ～ **11** のように表示しています。

② パソコンで音声データダウンロード（MP3）

［ご利用方法］

1 Web特典にアクセス　詳細は，p.7をご覧ください。

2 「一次試験［二次試験］音声データダウンロード」から
聞きたい検定の回を選択してダウンロード

※音声ファイルはzip形式にまとめられた形でダウンロードされます。
※音声の再生にはMP3を再生できる機器などが必要です。ご使用機器，音声再生ソフト等に関する技術的なご質問は，ハードメーカーもしくはソフトメーカーにお願いいたします。

③ スマートフォン・タブレットでストリーミング再生

［ご利用方法］

1 自動採点サービスにアクセス　詳細は，p.8をご覧ください。
（右のQRコードから読み込めます）

2 聞きたい検定の回を選び，
リスニングテストの音声再生ボタンを押す

※自動採点サービスは一次試験に対応していますので，一次試験・リスニングの音声のみお聞きいただけます。（二次試験・面接の音声をお聞きになりたい方は，①リスニングアプリ「英語の友」，②音声データダウンロードをご利用ください）
※音声再生中に音声を止めたい場合は，一時停止ボタンを押してください。
※個別に問題を再生したい場合は，問題番号を選んでから再生ボタンを押してください。
※音声の再生には多くの通信量が必要となりますので，Wi-Fi環境でのご利用をおすすめいたします。

Web特典について

購入者限定の「Web特典」を，皆さんの英検合格にお役立てください。

ご利用可能期間	2020年2月20日～2021年8月31日	
	※本サービスは予告なく変更，終了することがあります。	
アクセス方法	スマートフォン タブレット	右のQRコードを読み込むと，パスワードなしでアクセスできます！
	PC スマートフォン タブレット 共通	1. Web特典（以下のURL）にアクセスします。 https://eiken.obunsha.co.jp/3q/ 2. 本書を選択し，以下のパスワードを入力します。 avtphc ※すべて半角アルファベット小文字

〈特典内容〉

(1)自動採点サービス

リーディング（筆記1～3），リスニング（第1部～第3部）の自動採点ができます。詳細はp.8を参照してください。

(2) 解答用紙

本番にそっくりの解答用紙が印刷できるので，何度でも過去問にチャレンジすることができます。

(3)音声データのダウンロード

一次試験リスニング・二次試験面接の音声データ（MP3）を無料でダウンロードできます。

(4)3級面接対策

【面接シミュレーション】入室から退室までの面接の流れが体験できます。本番の面接と同じ手順で練習ができるので，実際に声に出して練習してみましょう。

【面接模範例】入室から退室までの模範応答例を見ることができます。各チェックポイントで，受験上の注意点やアドバイスを確認しておきましょう。

【問題カード】面接シミュレーションで使用している問題カードです。印刷して，実際の面接の練習に使ってください。

自動採点サービスの利用方法

正答率や合格ラインとの距離，間違えた問題の確認などができるサービスです。

ご利用可能期間	2020年2月20日～2021年8月31日		
	※本サービスは予告なく変更，終了することがあります。		
アクセス方法	スマートフォンタブレット	右のQRコードを読み込んでアクセスし，採点する検定の回を選択してください。	
	PCスマートフォンタブレット共通	p.7の手順で「Web特典」にアクセスし，「自動採点サービスを使う」を選択してご利用ください。	

〈利用方法〉

① オンラインマークシートにアクセスします。
② 「問題をはじめる」ボタンを押して試験を始めます。
③ 「答え合わせ」ボタンを選択します。
④ 【正答率・順位】（右画面）が表示されます。

〈採点結果の見方〉

タブの選択で【正答率・順位】と【問題ごとの正誤】が切り替えられます。

【正答率・順位】

Ⓐ技能ごとの正答率が表示されます。3級の合格の目安，正答率60%を目指しましょう。
Ⓑ大問ごとの正答率が表示されます。合格ラインを下回る問題は，対策に力を入れましょう。
Ⓒ採点サービス利用者の中でのあなたの順位が示されます。

【問題ごとの正誤】

各問題のあなたの解答と正解が表示されます。間違っている問題については色で示されますので，別冊解答の解説を見直しましょう。

〈採点結果画面〉　切り替えタブ

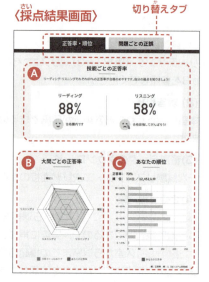

二次試験・面接の流れ

(1) 入室とあいさつ

係員の指示に従い，面接室に入ります。あいさつをしてから，面接委員に面接カードを手渡し，指示に従って，着席しましょう。

(2) 氏名と受験級の確認

面接委員があなたの氏名と受験する級の確認をします。その後，簡単なあいさつをしてから試験開始です。

(3) 問題カードの黙読

英文とイラストが印刷された問題カードを手渡されます。まず，英文を20秒で黙読するよう指示されます。英文の分量は30語程度です。

※問題カードには複数の種類があり，面接委員によっていずれか1枚が手渡されます。本書では英検協会から提供を受けたもののみ掲載しています。

(4) 問題カードの音読

英文の音読をするように指示されるので，英語のタイトルから読みましょう。時間制限はないので，意味のまとまりごとにポーズをとり，焦らずにゆっくりと読みましょう。

(5) 5つの質問

音読の後，面接委員の5つの質問に答えます。No.1～3は問題カードの英文とイラストについての質問です。No.4・5は受験者自身についての質問です。No.3の質問の後，カードを裏返すように指示されるので，No.4・5は面接委員を見ながら話しましょう。

(6) カード返却と退室

試験が終了したら，問題カードを面接委員に返却し，あいさつをして退室しましょう。

※二次試験にはA日程とB日程がありますが，受験級・申込方法・年齢・希望受験地等により，どちらかを指定されます。日程を選択・変更することはできません。詳しくは英検ウェブサイトをご確認ください。

9

英検®Information
インフォメーション

資料提供：公益財団法人 日本英語検定協会

英検3級について

3級では、「身近な英語を理解し、また使用できる」ことが求められます。3級の二次試験では、面接委員との対面式のスピーキングテストが実施されます。目安としては「中学卒業程度」です。

※2020年1月15日現在の情報です。
　最新情報は英検ウェブサイトをご確認ください。

合格すると…

英検Can-doリスト(英検合格者の実際の英語使用に対する自信の度合い)より

📖 読む
簡単な物語や身近なことに関する文章を理解することができる。

🔊 聞く
ゆっくり話してもらえば、身近なことに関する話や指示を理解することができる。

💬 話す
身近なことについて簡単なやりとりをしたり、自分のことについて述べることができる。

✏️ 書く
自分のことについて簡単な文章を書くことができる。

試験内容

一次試験　筆記・リスニング

主な場面・状況	家庭・学校・地域(各種店舗・公共施設を含む)・電話・アナウンスなど
主な話題	家族・友達・学校・趣味・旅行・買い物・スポーツ・映画・音楽・食事・天気・道案内・自己紹介・休日の予定・近況報告・海外の文化・人物紹介・歴史など

筆記試験 ⏱50分

問題	形式・課題詳細	問題数	満点スコア
1	短文の空所に文脈に合う適切な語句を補う。	15問	
2	会話文の空所に適切な文や語句を補う。	5問	550
3	パッセージ(長文)の内容に関する質問に答える。	10問	
4	与えられた質問に対して自分の考えとその裏付けとなる理由を書く。(25〜35語)	1問	550

リスニング ⏱約25分

問題	形式・課題詳細	問題数	満点スコア
第1部	会話の最後の発話に対する応答として最も適切なものを補う。(放送回数1回、補助イラスト付き)	10問	
第2部	会話の内容に関する質問に答える。(放送回数2回)	10問	550
第3部	短いパッセージの内容に関する質問に答える。(放送回数2回)	10問	

主な場面・題材 ｜ 身近なことに関する話題

過去の出題例 ｜ 携帯電話・ラジオを聴く・読書週間・冬のスポーツ・朝市・四季など

スピーキングテスト ⏱約5分	問題	形式・課題詳細	満点スコア
	音読	30語程度のパッセージを読む。	
	No.1	音読したパッセージの内容についての質問に答える。	
	No.2 No.3	イラスト中の人物の行動や物の状況を描写する。	550
	No.4 No.5	日常生活の身近な事柄についての質問に答える。（カードのトピックに直接関連しない内容も含む）	

▼4種類の英検®

英検には、実施方式が異なる4種類の試験があります。実施時期や受験上の配慮など、自分に合った方式を選択しましょう。なお、従来型の英検とその他の英検の**問題形式、難易度、級認定、合格証明書発行、英検CSEスコア取得等はすべて同じです。**

英検®(従来型)	紙の問題冊子を見て解答用紙に解答。二次試験（S）を受験するためには、一次試験（RLW）に合格する必要があります。
英検CBT®	コンピュータを使って1日で4技能を受験。Sはコンピュータを使った録音式で実施されます。
英検 2020 1 day S-CBT®	RLWは解答用紙に記入、Sはコンピュータを使った録音式。1日で4技能を受験することができます。
英検 2020 2 days S-Interview®	点字や吃音等、CBT方式では対応が難しい受験上の配慮が必要な方のみが受験可能。

RはReading、LはListening、WはWriting、SはSpeakingを表します。

受験する級によって選択できる方式が異なります。各方式の詳細および最新情報は英検ウェブサイト（https://www.eiken.or.jp/eiken/）をご確認ください。

❖ 合否判定方法

統計的に算出される英検CSEスコアに基づいて合否判定されます。Reading、Writing、Listening、Speakingの4技能が均等に評価され、合格基準スコアは固定されています。

■ 技能別にスコアが算出される！

技　能	試験形式	満点スコア	合格基準スコア
Reading（読む）	一次試験（筆記1〜3）	550	1103
Writing（書く）	一次試験（筆記4）	550	
Listening（聞く）	一次試験（リスニング）	550	
Speaking（話す）	二次試験（面接）	550	353

● 一次試験の合否は、Reading、Writing、Listeningの技能別にスコアが算出され、それを合算して判定されます。
● 二次試験の合否は、Speakingのみで判定されます。

■ 合格するためには、技能のバランスが重要！

英検CSEスコアでは、技能ごとに問題数は異なりますが、スコアを均等に配分しているため、各技能のバランスが重要となります。なお、正答数の目安を提示することはできませんが、2016年度第1回一次試験では、1級、準1級は各技能での正答率が7割程度、2級以下は各技能6割程度の正答率の受験者の多くが合格されています。

■ 英検CSEスコアは国際標準規格CEFRにも対応している！

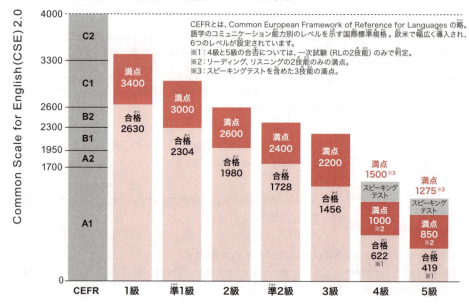

12

◇ 英検®（従来型）受験情報

■ 2020年度 試験日程

	第1回	第2回	第3回
申込受付	3月13日▶4月28日 (4月24日 書店締切)	8月3日▶9月10日 (9月4日 書店締切)	11月20日▶12月10日 (12月4日 書店締切)
一次試験	5月31日（日）	10月11日（日）	1月24日（日）2021年
二次試験	A 6月28日（日） B 7月5日（日）	A 11月8日（日） B 11月15日（日）	A 2月21日（日）2021年 B 2月28日（日）2021年

※二次試験にはA日程、B日程があり、条件により協会が指定します（日程の選択は不可）。詳しくは英検ウェブサイトをご覧ください。

■ 申込方法

団体受験：学校や塾などで申し込みをする団体受験もあります。詳しくは先生にお尋ねください。
個人受験：下記いずれかの方法でお申し込みください。

インターネット（願書不要）	英検ウェブサイトから直接申し込む。検定料は、クレジットカード、コンビニ、郵便局ATM、楽天ペイで支払う。
コンビニ（願書不要）	ローソン、ミニストップ、セブン-イレブン、ファミリーマートの店頭の情報端末に入力し、「申込券」が出力されたら検定料をレジで支払う。
英検特約書店（要願書）	書店で検定料を支払い、「書店払込証書」と「願書」を協会へ郵送。

※申込方法は変更になる場合があります。

■ 検定料

1級	準1級	2級	準2級	3級	4級	5級
10,300円	8,400円	7,400円	6,900円	**5,900円**	3,600円	3,000円

（本会場料金/税込）※検定料は変更になる場合があります。

※ 1～3級の「一次免除者（一次試験に合格し、二次試験を棄権または不合格になった人は、一次試験を1年間免除され、二次試験から受験することができる）」の検定料は、通常の受験者と同額です。

お問い合わせ先

英検サービスセンター	☎ **03-3266-8311**	月〜金 9:30〜17:00 （祝日・年末年始を除く）

英検ウェブサイト	**www.eiken.or.jp/eiken/**	試験についての詳しい情報を見たり、入試等で英検を活用している学校の検索をすることができます。

2019年度の傾向と攻略ポイント

2019年度第1回検定と第2回検定を分析し、出題傾向と攻略ポイントをまとめました。3級の合格に必要な正答率は6割程度と予測されます。正答率が6割を切った大問は苦手な分野だと考えましょう。

一次試験　筆記（50分）

1　短文の語句空所補充

短文または会話文中の空所に適切な語（句）を補う。

問題数 **15問**
めやす **10分**

傾向

単語 7問で、名詞（meaning, key など）、動詞（count, receive など）、形容詞（boring, peaceful, dirty など）、副詞（below, instead）が出題された。

熟語 5問で、Why don't you ～?, between A and B, take off ～, be proud of ～, the same as ～, be interested in ～, each other などが出題された。

文法 3問で、〈how to＋動詞の原形〉、名詞を修飾する現在分詞（動詞の～ing）、目的を表す to 不定詞〈to＋動詞の原形〉、疑問詞 who などが出題された。

攻略ポイント

単語は、問題文の意味をできるだけ正確に把握し、空所にどのような語が入れば意味が通じるかを考える。熟語は、特に空所前後にある語句とのつながりに注意する。文法は、文の意味や空所前後の語句との関係などから正しい語や形を判断する。

2　会話文の文空所補充

会話文中の空所に適切な文または文の一部を補う。

問題数 **5問**
めやす **5分**

傾向

A-B または A-B-A の会話文。解答のポイントとして、心配しないように伝える Don't worry., 聞いたことがあるかどうかを問う Have you heard of ～?, 提案をする What about ～?, 頻度を尋ねる How often ～? などの表現が含まれていた。

攻略ポイント

会話文全体の流れをつかむとともに、特に空所の前後でどのような発話がされているかをよく確認する。この問題では、自分が空所を含む方の話者になったつもりで対話文を読み、どのように応答すれば話が自然につながるかを考えてみよう。

3　長文の内容一致選択

[A] [B] [C] 3種類の英文を読んで内容に関する質問に答える。

問題数 **10問**
めやす **20分**

傾向

[A] は掲示で、フェスティバルを行う映画館の掲示、学校から保護者へのお知らせ。
[B] はEメールまたは手紙で、洗車でお金を得ることを考えているマイクと祖母とのEメール、学校を離れる先生へのプレゼントについて3人がやり取りしているE

メール。[C] は長文で，アイスホッケー選手のモーリス・リシャールに関する英文，ニューヨーク市のグランドセントラルターミナルに関する英文が出題された。

攻略ポイント [A] の掲示は，質問で求められている情報を，質問中の表現に注目して探し出す。[B] のＥメール・手紙と [C] の長文では，最初に質問を読んで読解のポイントを絞る。英文の各段落の概要を把握しながら，質問に関係する部分はていねいに読む。

---

4 英作文（ライティング）

英語で与えられた QUESTION について，自分の考えとその理由2つを 25 語〜35 語の英文で書く。

| 問題数 | **1問** |
| めやす | **15分** |

傾向 日常生活に関する身近な話題について QUESTION が出され，自分の考えと，その理由2つを 25 語〜35 語程度の英文で書く。話題として，「週のうちで何曜日が一番好きか」，「ご飯とパンのどちらをより頻繁に食べるか」が出題された。

攻略ポイント QUESTION を正確に理解し，問われていることに対応した内容を，〔自分の考え〕→〔理由1〕→〔理由2〕という構成で書く。理由が自分の考えをサポートする内容になっているか，使用している単語・表現・文法が適切か，分量が 25 語〜35 語になっているかなどに注意する。

🔊 一次試験　リスニング（約25分）

| 第1部 | **会話の応答文選択** | イラストを参考に，会話の最後の発話に対する応答として適切なものを選ぶ。放送は1回。 | 問題数 **10問** |

| 第2部 | **会話の内容一致選択** | A–B–A–B の会話の内容に関する質問に答える。放送は2回。 | 問題数 **10問** |

| 第3部 | **文の内容一致選択** | 35 語前後の英文の内容に関する質問に答える。放送は2回。 | 問題数 **10問** |

傾向 第1部と第2部では，友だち同士，先生と生徒，親子，孫と祖父母の会話などが出題された。第3部では，犬の世話の依頼，誕生日プレゼント，自分の生い立ち，仕事内容などが話題の英文に加え，ハイキングツアーの案内や野球場でのアナウンスも出題された。

攻略ポイント 第1部ではイラストから状況を把握し，どの選択肢が最後の発話に対応しているかを考える。第2部，第3部では選択肢を放送前に見て手がかりを得ておく。1回目の放送で話題・概要と質問を理解し，2回目は質問に関係する部分に注意して聞く。

15

二次試験　面接（約5分）

英文（パッセージ）とイラストの付いたカードが渡される。20秒の黙読の後，英文の音読をするよう指示される。それから，5つの質問がされる。

No. 1 問題カードにある英文の内容に関する質問。質問の主語を代名詞に置き換えて文を始めるとともに，質問に関係のない部分まで答えてしまわないように気をつける。

No. 2, 3 イラストについて，現在の動作（What is ～ doing?），これからの動作（What is ～ going to do?），数（How many ～?），場所（Where is [are] ～?）などが問われる。

No. 4, 5 受験者自身に関する質問。No.4 は今晩の予定や毎晩の睡眠時間などに関する質問。No.5 の質問は 2 つで，最初の質問には Yes ／ No で答えることが多い。2 番目の質問は，Yes の場合は Please tell me more. や Why? など，No の場合は Why not? のほか，最初の質問とは違う話題を聞かれることも多い。

Grade 3

2019-2

一次試験 2019.10. 6 実施
二次試験 A日程 2019.11. 3 実施
　　　　 B日程 2019.11.10実施

試験時間

筆記：50分
リスニング：約25分

2019年度第2回　**Web特典「自動採点サービス」対応**
オンラインマークシート
※検定の回によってQRコードが違います。
※筆記1〜3，リスニングの採点ができます。
※ PC からも利用できます（本書 p.8 参照）。

1 次の (1) から (15) までの (   ) に入れるのに最も適切なものを 1, 2, 3, 4 の中から一つ選び，その番号のマーク欄をぬりつぶしなさい。

(1) **A:** It's too cold to go swimming.
    B: I know. Let's stay home and watch TV (   ).
    1 either   **2** almost   **3** instead   **4** before

(2) Can you tell me the (   ) of this French word? I don't understand it.
    1 dictionary   **2** size   **3** meaning   **4** reason

(3) **A:** Excuse me. I want to try on this coat. Where's the (   ) room?
    B: It's over there, sir.
    1 putting   **2** picking   **3** hitting   **4** fitting

(4) It was a quiet and (   ) night, so I slept very well.
    1 close   **2** angry   **3** peaceful   **4** difficult

(5) **A:** Mom, I want to take a shower. Are there any clean (   )?
    B: Yes, Bobby. There are some in the bathroom.
    1 maps   **2** floors   **3** handles   **4** towels

(6) **A:** Are you looking for something, Jun?
    B: Yes, my bicycle (   ). I've looked in all my pockets and my bag.
    1 type   **2** line   **3** job   **4** key

(7) **A:** Jack. Clean your shoes before you go to school. They're (   ).
    B: All right, Mom. I'll do it.
    1 dirty   **2** sick   **3** thirsty   **4** round

(8) Tom's parents were very proud (   ) him when he passed his exam.

  1 by   **2** of   **3** on   **4** from

(9) My new telephone is just the (   ) as my brother's.

  1 different   **2** same   **3** true   **4** more

(10) Michael is (   ) in computers, but he doesn't have one.

  1 excited   **2** interested   **3** difficult   **4** free

(11) *A:* Where did your parents first meet (   ) other?

  B: They met in junior high school.

  1 each   **2** so   **3** every   **4** many

(12) My father broke his (   ). He couldn't take us to the beach on Saturday because he had to work.

  1 pollution   **2** promise   **3** problem   **4** purpose

(13) John went to school early today (   ) volleyball.

  1 to practice   **2** practiced   **3** practice   **4** practices

(14) *A:* Do you know (   ) made this pumpkin pie? It's delicious!

  B: Patty did. She's a great cook.

  1 when   **2** who   **3** what   **4** how

(15) *A:* Fumiko, your brother goes to university, (   ) he?

  B: Yes, he's graduating this year.

  1 wasn't   **2** doesn't   **3** won't   **4** can't

(16) *Salesclerk:* Good afternoon, sir. Can I help you?
 Customer: No, thanks. I'm just looking.
 Salesclerk: All right. Please tell me ( )
 1 if I have one. **2** when it will arrive.
 3 if you need me. **4** when you can come.

(17) *Man:* Why don't we go out to dinner tonight?
 Woman: OK. ( )
 Man: Sounds good.
 1 What about Italian food? **2** Let's eat at home.
 3 Can you pass the salt? **4** I'll clean the table.

(18) *Husband:* Do you like any of the raincoats in this shop?
 Wife: ( ) I think I'll buy it.
 1 It rains a lot during winter.
 2 It was a gift from my sister.
 3 The red one by the entrance is nice.
 4 The sale finished last weekend.

(19) *Girl 1:* I didn't know you had a violin. ( )
 Girl 2: Only once or twice a month.
 1 When did you get it? **2** How often do you play it?
 3 Was it a present? **4** Is it an expensive one?

(20) *Boy:* Hurry up, Christine. We need to go to English class.
 Girl: ( ) I have to get my dictionary from my locker.
 1 Three lessons a week. **2** Just a little.
 3 I know the answer. **4** Wait a minute.

（筆記試験の問題は次のページに続きます。）

Notice to Parents

The 8th grade students are going to grow some vegetables at school for their science class. Some students will come to school on May 28 to get the garden ready, and we're looking for five parents to come and help them.

> **Date:** Saturday, May 28
> **Time:** 10 a.m. to 3 p.m.
> **Where:** Meet beside the school pool
> **What to bring:** Something to eat and drink

You need to be strong because there will be many heavy things to carry.

If you can help, please call Mr. Clark, the science teacher, at 344-2323 by May 24.

(21) On May 28, the parents should meet

    1 at the supermarket.
    2 outside Mr. Clark's classroom.
    3 next to the school pool.
    4 in the science room.

(22) What will the parents have to do at the school?

    1 Teach a science class.
    2 Make drinks for the students.
    3 Sell vegetables.
    4 Carry heavy things.

From: Amanda Jarvis
To: George Wilson, Donna Thompson
Date: February 10
Subject: Mr. Ward

Hi George and Donna,
I still can't believe Mr. Ward is leaving our school. He's such a good teacher! I talked to him this afternoon, and he said his wife found a new job at a university in Boston. He said they were going to move there soon. I'm really sad about it, but I hope he enjoys living in Boston. I think his daughter will have a lot of fun there. Donna, at lunchtime today, you said we should buy Mr. Ward a present. I think that's a great idea.
See you soon,
Amanda

From: George Wilson
To: Amanda Jarvis, Donna Thompson
Date: February 11
Subject: Good idea

Hello,
I think getting a present is a good idea, too. Mr. Ward has always been kind to us, so we should give him something nice. I know he likes all sports, but I heard that he loves soccer the best. He enjoys reading, too, so how about a book about soccer? Also, we should ask everyone in our class to help. If everyone gives a little money, we'll be able to get him something really special.
George

From: Donna Thompson
To: George Wilson, Amanda Jarvis
Date: February 11
Subject: Gift

Hi George and Amanda,
I agree with George. Let's ask our classmates to help. If everyone gives $5, we'll have $100. Then, we can buy him something better than a book. His favorite soccer team is the Panthers, right? I saw a really cool Panthers clock on the Internet the other day. It was about $100. If we can collect enough money, I think we should buy him that. What do you think?
See you on Monday,
Donna

(23) Why is Mr. Ward going to move?

    1 He will stop teaching.
    2 He wants to go back to university.
    3 His daughter lives in Boston.
    4 His wife got a new job.

(24) What did George hear about Mr. Ward?

    1 His favorite sport is soccer.
    2 He has a lot of nice things.
    3 His classes are really boring.
    4 He wrote a book about soccer.

(25) What does Donna want to give Mr. Ward?

    1 Some money.
    2 A clock.
    3 A soccer ball.
    4 A book.

Grand Central Terminal

One of New York City's most famous symbols is Grand Central Terminal. This is the city's main train station. About 750,000 people walk through it every day.

When the station was first built in 1871 by a man named Cornelius Vanderbilt, it was called Grand Central Depot. In 1901, a larger building was built and named Grand Central Station. However, that building was closed because of a big train accident in 1902. In 1913, a new and even bigger station was opened, and it was given the name Grand Central Terminal. This is the one that people can still see today.

Grand Central Terminal has 44 platforms.* That is more than any other train station in the world. It also has 67 train tracks.* The main hall is called the Main Concourse, and it is very big. The windows are about 23 meters high. The Main Concourse has many interesting things to look at. In the middle, there is a famous clock made of opal. Opal is a very expensive stone, so it cost millions of dollars. Many people meet their friends by the clock.

On the ceiling* of the Main Concourse, there is a picture of the night sky with 2,500 bright stars. This ceiling was made in 1912, but it was covered in 1944 because it was old and rainwater was coming into the building. From 1996 to 1998, the ceiling was cleaned and fixed. Now, it is one of the most beautiful parts of the building.

*platform：(駅の) ホーム
*track：線路
*ceiling：天井

(26) In 1871, the name of New York City's main train station was

    1 Grand Central Terminal.
    2 Grand Central Station.
    3 Grand Central Depot.
    4 the Main Concourse.

(27) What happened in 1902?

    1 Grand Central Depot was built.
    2 There was a bad accident at Grand Central Station.
    3 A new Grand Central Terminal was opened.
    4 A man named Cornelius Vanderbilt was born.

(28) Why did the clock cost millions of dollars?

    1 It has many stars with bright lights in it.
    2 It has a picture of famous people on it.
    3 It is made of an expensive stone.
    4 It is 23 meters high.

(29) What was cleaned and fixed in the Main Concourse?

    1 The ceiling.
    2 The platforms.
    3 The clock.
    4 The windows.

(30) What is this story about?

    1 Traveling around the United States by train.
    2 The life of Cornelius Vanderbilt.
    3 A new art museum in New York City.
    4 A famous place in New York City.

ライティング

4

- ● あなたは，外国人の友達から以下のQUESTIONをされました。
- ● QUESTIONについて，あなたの考えとその<u>理由を2つ</u>英文で書きなさい。
- ● 語数の目安は25語〜35語です。
- ● 解答は，解答用紙のＢ面にあるライティング解答欄に書きなさい。<u>なお，解答欄の外に書かれたものは採点されません。</u>
- ● <u>解答がQUESTIONに対応していないと判断された場合は，0点と採点されることがあります。</u>QUESTIONをよく読んでから答えてください。

QUESTION

Which do you eat more often, rice or bread?

一次試験

リスニング

３級リスニングテストについて

1 このテストには，第1部から第3部まであります。
☆英文は第1部では一度だけ，第2部と第3部では二度，放送されます。
第1部：イラストを参考にしながら対話と応答を聞き，最も適切な応答を 1, 2, 3 の中から一つ選びなさい。
第2部：対話と質問を聞き，その答えとして最も適切なものを 1, 2, 3, 4 の中から一つ選びなさい。
第3部：英文と質問を聞き，その答えとして最も適切なものを 1, 2, 3, 4 の中から一つ選びなさい。

2 No. 30 のあと，10 秒すると試験終了の合図がありますので，筆記用具を置いてください。

第1部 🔊 ▶MP3 ▶アプリ ▶CD1 **1**～**11**

〔例題〕

No. 1

No. 2

No. 3

No. 4

No. 5

No. 6

No. 7

No. 8

No. 9

No. 10

No. 11	1 At 12:15 p.m.
	2 At 12:50 p.m.
	3 At 1:00 p.m.
	4 At 1:45 p.m.

No. 12	1 Play tennis with Meg.
	2 Watch tennis on TV.
	3 Go shopping with Meg.
	4 Buy a new tennis racket.

No. 13	1 It was too expensive.
	2 He was far from the mountains.
	3 He had a bad headache.
	4 There wasn't enough snow.

No. 14	1 Play with a friend.
	2 Visit a zoo.
	3 Go to his grandfather's house.
	4 Go on a trip with his friends.

No. 15	1 Eat breakfast.
	2 Get her books.
	3 Brush her teeth.
	4 Wash her face.

No. 16	1 One dollar.
	2 Four dollars.
	3 Ten dollars.
	4 Fifteen dollars.

No. 17	1 The girl.
	2 The girl's brother.
	3 The girl's mother.
	4 The girl's grandmother.

No. 18	1 In a library.
	2 In a convenience store.
	3 In a post office.
	4 In a bank.

No. 19	1 Pick up Sam.
	2 Clean the house.
	3 Buy dinner.
	4 Call her friend.

No. 20	1 Her passport.
	2 Her ticket.
	3 Her watch.
	4 Her car keys.

No. 21
1 Going fishing.
2 Buying lunch.
3 His father's job.
4 His favorite fish.

No. 22
1 For one week.
2 For three weeks.
3 For one year.
4 For three years.

No. 23
1 His friend.
2 His friend's parents.
3 His father.
4 His grandfather.

No. 24
1 In Australia.
2 In Canada.
3 In Europe.
4 In Asia.

No. 25
1 He is a carpenter.
2 He is an actor.
3 He is a cook.
4 He is a teacher.

No. 26
1 15.
2 50.
3 85.
4 100.

No. 27	1 To buy a book.
	2 To ask about a job.
	3 To look for a magazine.
	4 To meet a writer.

No. 28	1 Tom saw a snake.
	2 Tom watched a scary movie.
	3 Tom cleaned his house.
	4 Tom got lost in the forest.

No. 29	1 At 1:00.
	2 At 5:30.
	3 At 6:00.
	4 At 6:30.

No. 30	1 She took some art classes.
	2 She visited France.
	3 She met her husband's family.
	4 She studied Italian.

問題カード（A 日程）　　🔊 ▶ MP3 ▶ アプリ ▶ CD1 34～38

International Supermarkets

There are many international supermarkets in Japan. International supermarkets sell interesting food from different countries, so they are popular with many people. The food at these stores is sometimes expensive.

Questions

No. 1   Please look at the passage.   Why are international supermarkets popular with many people?

No. 2   Please look at the picture.   Where are the cups?

No. 3   Please look at the man wearing a hat.   What is he doing?

Now, Mr. / Ms. ——, please turn the card over.

No. 4   What are you planning to do this evening?

No. 5   Do you have any pets?
　　　　　　Yes. → Please tell me more.
　　　　　　No. → What kind of pet would you like to have?

Concerts

Watching famous singers or bands on stage is exciting. Many people enjoy going to concerts with their friends, but some people like watching concerts alone. Music festivals are often held outside in summer.

Questions

No. 1   Please look at the passage. What do some people like doing?

No. 2   Please look at the picture. What does the man have in his hands?

No. 3   Please look at the woman with long hair. What is she doing?

Now, Mr. / Ms. ——, please turn the card over.

No. 4   How many hours do you sleep every night?

No. 5   Do you enjoy watching TV?
        Yes. → Please tell me more.
        No. → What do you like to do after dinner?

2019-1

一次試験 2019.6.2 実施
二次試験　A日程　2019.6.30実施
　　　　　B日程　2019.7.7 実施

Grade 3

試験時間

筆記：50分
リスニング：約25分

2019年度第1回　**Web特典「自動採点サービス」対応**
オンラインマークシート
※検定の回によってQRコードが違います。
※筆記1〜3，リスニングの採点ができます。
※ PC からも利用できます（本書 p.8 参照）。

1 次の (1) から (15) までの (　　) に入れるのに最も適切なものを 1, 2, 3, 4 の中から一つ選び, その番号のマーク欄をぬりつぶしなさい。

(1) *A:* Do you like to go fishing?
B: No, I think fishing is (　　).
1 boring　　**2** exciting　　**3** enjoyable　　**4** glad

(2) Andy lives on the sixth floor of a big building. His friend David lives in the apartment (　　) on the fifth floor.
1 back　　**2** below　　**3** before　　**4** later

(3) *A:* How many pens are in this box?
B: I don't know. Let's (　　) them and find out.
1 invite　　**2** break　　**3** turn　　**4** count

(4) *A:* You have a beautiful home, Clara.
B: Thank you. My father (　　) it.
1 designed　　**2** brought　　**3** shared　　**4** wrote

(5) The football game begins at 7:00, so let's (　　) outside the station at 6:15.
1 meet　　**2** make　　**3** come　　**4** show

(6) When you speak in front of many people, you must speak in a (　　) voice.
1 tall　　**2** long　　**3** loud　　**4** wide

(7) If you win the art contest, you will (　　) a prize.
1 invite　　**2** guess　　**3** receive　　**4** serve

42

(8) *A:* I got two tickets for the baseball game. (　　　) don't you come with me?

B: Sounds great. I really want to go.

1 How　　　　**2** Why　　　　**3** What　　　　**4** When

(9) I usually get up at seven o'clock and go to bed (　　　) nine and ten.

1 before　　　**2** on　　　　**3** still　　　　**4** between

(10) Nancy wants to save money, so she will not go (　　　) to eat this week.

1 near　　　　**2** out　　　　**3** by　　　　　**4** down

(11) We (　　　) a lot of fun when my parents took us camping last weekend.

1 had　　　　**2** did　　　　**3** played　　　**4** got

(12) At my school, people must (　　　) off their shoes when they go into the school building.

1 have　　　　**2** make　　　　**3** take　　　　**4** bring

(13) My brother is a musician. He is going to teach me (　　　) to play the guitar.

1 how　　　　**2** who　　　　**3** that　　　　**4** what

(14) If Frank (　　　) his knee in today's practice, he won't be able to play in the soccer tournament on the weekend.

1 injure　　　**2** injures　　　**3** injuring　　　**4** to injure

(15) *A:* Look at the monkey (　　　) a banana over there.

B: Oh, it's really cute.

1 to eat　　　**2** ate　　　　**3** eating　　　**4** eats

(16) *Daughter:* I hope I do well on my final exam today.

    Mother: (　　　　) You studied hard, so you'll do well.

1 Don't worry.　　　　　　　　**2** I don't have a dictionary.

3 That's your teacher.　　　　　**4** All weekend.

(17) *Woman:* I went to a restaurant called Mama Dell's last night.
(　　　)

    Man: Yes.　My friend said it's delicious.

1 Have you heard of it?　　　　**2** Are you finished?

3 May I come in?　　　　　　　**4** What did you buy?

(18) *Father:* How are you feeling today, Paul?

    Son: (　　　　) I still have a fever.

1 After I have breakfast.　　　　**2** Not at the moment.

3 Not so good.　　　　　　　　**4** If I have time.

(19) *Daughter:* Can you take me to the park, Mom?

    Mother: (　　　　) Let's watch a movie instead.

1 I don't know that actor.　　　　**2** Come back before dinner.

3 I've seen it before.　　　　　　**4** It's too cold to play outside.

(20)   *Man:* Aren't you going to Australia soon?

  Woman: Yeah.　(　　　　) so I have to get ready this weekend.

1 It was a wonderful trip,

2 I'm leaving on Monday morning,

3 I was born in Sydney,

4 I'll bring you back a present,

（筆記試験の問題は次のページに続きます。）

3[A]

Japanese Movie Festival

Come to Suntown Theater and enjoy some amazing Japanese movies! There will be comedies, dramas, horror movies, and a lot more.

When: July 10 to July 20

Where: Suntown Theater, 21 Wilson Street

Ticket Prices: Adults - $15   Students & Children - $10

You'll be given a free bottle of Japanese green tea with each ticket.

On July 10, the festival will begin with a comedy called *Karaoke King*. The famous actor, Akira Sato, will come to the theater and talk about the movie before it starts. If you want to attend this event, buy a ticket soon!

Check our website for more information: www.suntowntheater.com

(21) What will people get when they buy a ticket?

    1 A Japanese snack.
    2 A *Karaoke King* DVD.
    3 A bottle of tea.
    4 A movie poster.

(22) What will happen on July 10?

    1 Akira Sato will give a talk about *Karaoke King*.
    2 The movie festival will finish.
    3 There will be a karaoke contest at Suntown Theater.
    4 Suntown Theater will be closed.

From: Mike Costello
To: Rose Costello
Date: June 25
Subject: New idea

Hi Grandma,

How are you? School finished last week, so I'm on summer vacation now. I play video games or go swimming at the pool every day. I asked Dad for some money to buy some new games, but he said no. He said I should find a part-time job. I'm 17 years old now, so I guess he's right. Anyway, I have an idea. I've decided to start my own business. I'm going to wash people's cars. I'll visit their houses and wash each car for $10. I've already asked some of Mom and Dad's friends, and they said they're interested. How about you, Grandma? Would you like me to wash your car sometime?

Love,
Mike

From: Rose Costello
To: Mike Costello
Date: June 25
Subject: This Saturday

Hello Mike,

Thank you for your e-mail. I'm glad to hear you're enjoying your summer vacation. Your mother called yesterday. She said she's worried because you didn't do well on your last math test. I'm sure you'll do better next time. That's a great idea for a business. Could you come and wash my car for me? Your grandfather usually does it, but he's getting old. It's very hard for him to do it these days. You can come and wash it once a month. Could you

48

come this Saturday at noon? I'll pay you, of course, but I'd also like to make you something to eat for lunch. How about tuna and cheese sandwiches? Please call me by Friday night and let me know.
Love,
Grandma

(23) What was Mike's problem at first?

    1 His father didn't give him money.
    2 He was too busy to find a new job.
    3 He didn't like his job at the pool.
    4 He couldn't swim well.

(24) What did Mike's mother say about Mike?

    1 He doesn't want to work for a famous car company.
    2 His favorite subject at school is math.
    3 He wants to go to a driving school this summer.
    4 He didn't get a good score on his math test.

(25) This Saturday, Mike's grandmother wants Mike to

    1 wash her car.
    2 make sandwiches.
    3 call his grandfather.
    4 drive her to the store.

次の英文の内容に関して，(26) から (30) までの質問に対する答えとして最も適切なもの，または文を完成させるのに最も適切なものを 1, 2, 3, 4 の中から一つ選び，その番号のマーク欄をぬりつぶしなさい。

Maurice Richard

In Canada, more children play soccer than any other sport, but ice hockey is also popular. Many children dream of becoming professional ice hockey players. For them, ice hockey players are special. One famous Canadian ice hockey player is Maurice Richard.

Maurice was born in 1921 in Montreal, Canada. When he was growing up, he enjoyed ice-skating, baseball, and boxing, but he loved ice hockey the most. When he was 14, he started playing ice hockey at school with his friends. He left school and got a job with his father when he was 16. Then, when he was 18, he joined an amateur* ice hockey team.

When Maurice was 21, he started playing for a professional ice hockey team called the Montreal Canadiens. Maurice soon became an important player on his team, and he was the first player to get 50 goals in one season. He was strong and skated very fast, so people started calling him "The Rocket." When he played, his team won many games. He helped the Montreal Canadiens to win the Stanley Cup* eight times. Maurice stopped playing ice hockey in 1960. He was a professional ice hockey player for 18 years.

When Maurice died in 2000, many Canadians were sad. People loved him because he was one of the greatest ice hockey players in history. He is still remembered because there is an award called the Maurice "Rocket" Richard Trophy. Every year, it is given to the player who gets the most goals in one season.

*amateur：アマチュア
*Stanley Cup：北米プロアイスホッケー優勝決定戦

(26) Which sport is played by the most children in Canada?

1 Boxing.
2 Soccer.
3 Baseball.
4 Ice hockey.

(27) What did Maurice Richard do when he was 16 years old?

1 He started playing ice hockey.
2 He joined a boxing club with his friends.
3 He started working with his father.
4 He joined an amateur ice hockey team.

(28) Why was Maurice called "The Rocket"?

1 He was very good at boxing.
2 His teammates loved him.
3 He was a strong and fast skater.
4 He played for the Montreal Canadiens.

(29) Maurice is still remembered because there is

1 a special award with his name.
2 a professional ice hockey team with his name.
3 a Canadian city with his name.
4 a skating school with his name.

(30) What is this story about?

1 A way to become a professional ice hockey player.
2 A famous Canadian ice hockey player.
3 An amateur ice hockey team in Canada.
4 A new award for young ice hockey players.

ライティング

4
- あなたは,外国人の友達から以下のQUESTIONをされました。
- QUESTIONについて,あなたの考えとその理由を2つ英文で書きなさい。
- 語数の目安は25語～35語です。
- 解答は,解答用紙のB面にあるライティング解答欄に書きなさい。なお,解答欄の外に書かれたものは採点されません。
- 解答がQUESTIONに対応していないと判断された場合は,0点と採点されることがあります。QUESTIONをよく読んでから答えてください。

QUESTION
What day of the week do you like the best?

リスニング

３級リスニングテストについて

1 このテストには，第1部から第3部まであります。
　☆英文は第1部では一度だけ，第2部と第3部では二度，放送されます。
　第1部：イラストを参考にしながら対話と応答を聞き，最も適切な応答を 1, 2, 3
　　　　の中から一つ選びなさい。
　第2部：対話と質問を聞き，その答えとして最も適切なものを 1, 2, 3, 4 の中から
　　　　一つ選びなさい。
　第3部：英文と質問を聞き，その答えとして最も適切なものを 1, 2, 3, 4 の中から
　　　　一つ選びなさい。
2 No. 30 のあと，10 秒すると試験終了の合図がありますので，筆記用具を置いてく
　ださい。

||||| 第 1 部 ||||||　🔊 ▶ MP3 ▶ アプリ ▶ CD 1 43〜53

〔例題〕

No. 1

No. 2

No. 3

No. 4

No. 5

No. 6

No. 7

No. 8

No. 9

No. 10

No. 11
1 At Jim's family's house.
2 At Jim's friend's house.
3 At a supermarket.
4 At a restaurant.

No. 12
1 Buy a cheesecake.
2 Make a cake herself.
3 Go to the store again.
4 Shop at a different store.

No. 13
1 Becky's father.
2 Becky's brother.
3 Jim's father.
4 Jim's brother.

No. 14
1 Take a train.
2 Go to a new bakery.
3 Make their lunch.
4 Visit their friend's house.

No. 15
1 Ken's new friend.
2 Ken's favorite band.
3 Ken's room.
4 Ken's weekend.

No. 16
1 The girl's team won its game.
2 The girl got a goal.
3 The boy went to a soccer game.
4 The coach was late.

No. 17	1 Yesterday morning.
	2 Last night.
	3 This morning.
	4 At lunchtime.

No. 18	1 He can't see the stars tonight.
	2 It will be cloudy tomorrow.
	3 He can't find the newspaper.
	4 His science homework is hard.

No. 19	1 Return the woman's money.
	2 Get a new washing machine.
	3 Buy a new house.
	4 Visit the woman next month.

No. 20	1 Five kilometers.
	2 Six kilometers.
	3 Ten kilometers.
	4 Thirty kilometers.

No. 21
1 On the train.
2 At the station.
3 By the tennis court.
4 At her house.

No. 22
1 Go on a trip.
2 Buy her a pet.
3 Take care of her dog.
4 Visit her grandparents.

No. 23
1 He went shopping.
2 He studied at home.
3 He helped his mother.
4 He worked at a restaurant.

No. 24
1 She couldn't find her brother.
2 She forgot her brother's birthday.
3 The bookstore wasn't open.
4 The book was too expensive.

No. 25
1 Visit his grandparents.
2 Go on a trip with his mother.
3 Teach English at a school.
4 Start learning Chinese.

No. 26
1 Some shoes.
2 A dress.
3 A wedding ring.
4 A hat.

No. 27

1 This morning.
2 On Friday evening.
3 On Saturday evening.
4 On Sunday morning.

No. 28

1 English.
2 Math.
3 Science.
4 Music.

No. 29

1 His sister's story was very good.
2 He met a famous writer.
3 His sister won a prize.
4 He found his library book.

No. 30

1 For fifteen minutes.
2 For thirty minutes.
3 For one hour.
4 For two hours.

A Popular Japanese Food

Tofu is used in many delicious Japanese dishes.　Some people like to put it in salad, soup, and even ice cream and cake.　Tofu is healthy and cheap, so it is eaten by many people.

Questions

No. 1   Please look at the passage. Why is tofu eaten by many people?

No. 2   Please look at the picture. How many bottles of water is the woman holding?

No. 3   Please look at the man with glasses. What is he going to do?

Now, Mr. / Ms. ——, please turn the card over.

No. 4   What do you do to relax in your free time?

No. 5   Have you ever been to a zoo?
             Yes. → Please tell me more.
             No. → Where do you like to go on weekends?

Health Clubs

In Japan, there are lots of health clubs. Many people want to stay strong and healthy, so they become members of health clubs. Sometimes, people can make new friends there, too.

Questions

No. 1   Please look at the passage. Why do many people become members of health clubs?

No. 2   Please look at the picture. Where is the television?

No. 3   Please look at the woman. What is she going to do?

Now, Mr. / Ms. ——, please turn the card over.

No. 4   What kind of movies do you like to watch?

No. 5   Do you like to eat at restaurants?

    Yes. → Please tell me more.

    No. → Why not?

2018-3

一次試験 2019.1.27実施
二次試験 A日程 2019.2.24実施
　　　　B日程 2019.3.3 実施

試験時間

筆記：**50分**
リスニング：**約25分**

一次試験・筆記　　　　　p.66〜76
一次試験・リスニング　　p.77〜82
二次試験・面接　　　　　p.84〜87

＊解答・解説は別冊p.77〜112にあります。
＊面接の流れは本書p.9にあります。

Grade 3

1 次の (1) から (15) までの ( ) に入れるのに最も適切なものを 1, 2, 3, 4 の中から一つ選び, その番号のマーク欄をぬりつぶしなさい。

(1) John has a good ( ). He can remember all his friends' phone numbers.

    1 care   **2** wish   **3** memory   **4** hope

(2) *A:* Mom, that box is really big. I'll ( ) it for you.
    B: Oh, thank you, Edward.

    1 enter   **2** guess   **3** believe   **4** carry

(3) Sally is a TV reporter. She was really excited today because she had an ( ) with a famous singer.

    1 answer   **2** example   **3** interview   **4** order

(4) *A:* Linda, are you ( ) for the party yet?
    B: No, I don't know what I should wear.

    1 needed   **2** signed   **3** moved   **4** dressed

(5) Christina is an actress. She is often on TV and sometimes ( ) on stage.

    1 invents   **2** performs   **3** protects   **4** imagines

(6) This clock was made early in the 20th ( ), so it's about 100 years old.

    1 area   **2** century   **3** moment   **4** tournament

(7) Matt usually leaves for work ( ) eating breakfast. He has toast and coffee at a coffee shop near the station.

    1 since   **2** between   **3** through   **4** without

(8) Karen's house is bigger than (   ) other house on her street.

1 own   **2** whole   **3** any   **4** much

(9) My grandfather loves jogging. It rained today, but he got up early and went jogging (   ) usual.

1 as   **2** ever   **3** by   **4** on

(10) *A:* Susan will graduate from nursing school next month.
B: I know. She really wants to be a nurse, and now her dream will (   ) true at last.

1 come   **2** get   **3** go   **4** have

(11) *A:* What's the (   ), Shelly?
B: I lost my purse.

1 horizon   **2** matter   **3** difference   **4** figure

(12) *A:* It's dark in here. Could you turn (   ) the light, Sam?
B: Sure.

1 off   **2** with   **3** in   **4** on

(13) Jack finished (   ) his room and then went to his friend's house.

1 clean   **2** cleaned   **3** cleaning   **4** cleans

(14) *A:* It's Tom's birthday next Saturday. Let's (   ) him a present.
B: Good idea.

1 buy   **2** buys   **3** to buy   **4** buying

(15) *A:* Sean is always late, (   ) he?
B: Yes. One time I waited two hours for him.

1 didn't   **2** isn't   **3** couldn't   **4** hasn't

2

次の (16) から (20) までの会話について, (　　　) に入れるのに最も適切なもの
を 1, 2, 3, 4 の中から一つ選び, その番号のマーク欄をぬりつぶしなさい。

(16) **Wife:** Can you show me how to check my e-mail on the new computer?

Husband: (　　　) Mary.　I'm on the phone with my boss.

1 Just a minute,　　　　　　2 By the chair,

3 I checked my office,　　　4 I got a new one,

(17) **Girl:** Your dog is so cute.　How long have you had him?

Boy: (　　　)

1 Since I was five.

2 My grandma gave him to me.

3 About 10 kilograms.

4 For an hour every morning.

(18) **Woman:** Did you know that Paul Edwards got married last month?

Man: No.　(　　　)

Woman: His younger brother.

1 What did you give him?　　2 Was it a big wedding?

3 Who told you that?　　　　4 Have you met his wife?

(19) **Woman 1:** I have to go and buy some Christmas presents this weekend.

Woman 2: Me, too.　(　　　)

Woman 1: OK.　Sounds good.

1 Do you know what they want?

2 Why don't you return it?

3 Do you remember last year's party?

4 Why don't we go together?

(20) **Girl:** When's your big tennis match?

Boy: Tomorrow.　I haven't practiced much this week, so (　　　)

1 it starts at two o'clock.　　2 I'm a little worried.

3 it's going to rain.　　　　　4 I really like your racket.

（筆記試験の問題は次のページに続きます。）

次の掲示の内容に関して，(21) と (22) の質問に対する答えとして最も適切な
もの，または文を完成させるのに最も適切なものを 1, 2, 3, 4 の中から一つ選
び，その番号のマーク欄をぬりつぶしなさい。

Blue Sea Amusement

Whale Watching Boat Rides

Come and join a whale watching tour with us! If you don't see a whale, you can still enjoy the beautiful ocean and learn about the history of South Bay.

Boats leave every two hours from 10 a.m. to 4 p.m. The whale watching season is from May to September. We are closed every Tuesday and when the weather is bad.

Ticket Prices
✧ Adults: $35
✧ Children 3 to 12: $18
✧ Children under 3: free

If you want to have a special party on one of our boats, please check our website for more information:

www.blueseawhalewatching.com

(21) What is this notice about?

    1 A show at an amusement park.
    2 A class about the history of boats.
    3 A boat tour to see whales.
    4 A special party on the beach.

(22) People cannot go on a boat ride

    1 if they are under 12 years old.
    2 between 10 a.m. and 4 p.m.
    3 if the weather is bad.
    4 on Thursdays.

From: Nancy Hill
To: Junko Kobayashi
Date: May 12
Subject: Driving lessons

Hi Junko,
How are you? My summer vacation will start in three weeks. Last week, I took a driving class after school at my high school, and I'm going to take the driving test in the second week of June. If I pass the test, I can drive us around when you come in August. I want to take a trip to my grandmother's house when you're here. We can drive there.
I can't wait to see you!
Nancy

From: Junko Kobayashi
To: Nancy Hill
Date: May 13
Subject: Really?

Hi Nancy,
Thanks for your e-mail. My summer vacation doesn't start until the end of July. You're only 16, so I'm surprised that you can get a driver's license. In Japan, we have to be 18 years old. I'm planning to go to a driving school when I start university. Getting a driver's license is very expensive in Japan. How much does it cost in the United States? I think you'll be a good driver. Anyway, I would love to meet your grandmother.
Your friend,
Junko

From: Nancy Hill
To: Junko Kobayashi
Date: May 13
Subject: This summer

Hi Junko,
Wow, you can't get a driver's license until you're 18! Most people in the United States can get their driver's license when they're 16. I think it's also cheaper here. The class at my school was free. When I take the driving test, I only have to pay $40. On weekends, I drive near my house with my mom or dad. It's good practice. I can't drive by myself yet, so one of my parents has to be in the car with me.
Write again soon!
Nancy

(23) When will Junko visit Nancy?

    1 In three weeks.
    2 In the second week of June.
    3 At the end of July.
    4 In August.

(24) What is Junko planning to do when she starts university?

    1 Learn how to drive.
    2 Take a driving test in the United States.
    3 Take a special class at Nancy's school.
    4 Drive to her grandmother's house.

(25) How does Nancy practice driving on weekends?

    1 She drives by herself.
    2 She pays her teacher $40 for a lesson.
    3 She drives with one of her parents.
    4 She drives to her friend's house.

次の英文の内容に関して，(26) から (30) までの質問に対する答えとして最も適切なもの，または文を完成させるのに最も適切なものを 1, 2, 3, 4 の中から一つ選び，その番号のマーク欄をぬりつぶしなさい。

Valentinus

Many people around the world celebrate Valentine's Day. In some countries, people give chocolate or other gifts to friends and family. They do this to show their love for those people. However, the history of Valentine's Day is actually very sad. The name Valentine's Day comes from the name of a Roman priest* called Valentinus. He was born in the year 226.

In those days, Rome had a very large and strong army.* Many of the soldiers* in the army wanted to get married and have families. However, the leader of Rome, Claudius II, thought soldiers should not be married, so he made it a rule. After that, they could not get married anymore. Some soldiers broke the rule and got married, but they could not tell anyone.

Many priests were afraid of Claudius II, so they did not help soldiers to get married. However, Valentinus thought that men and women should get married and have families. So he helped soldiers when they wanted to get married. One day, when people found out Valentinus was doing this, he got in trouble and was put in jail.*

When Valentinus was in jail, he met a young girl who worked there. Every day, she brought food to Valentinus and talked with him, and they became good friends. But Claudius II decided to kill Valentinus. On the night before he died, Valentinus wrote a letter to the girl. He signed the letter, "Your Valentine." The next day, February 14, Valentinus was killed. However, today, many people celebrate love on this day.

*priest：神父
*army：軍隊
*soldier：兵士
*be put in jail：投獄される

(26) Valentine's Day was named after

    1 a famous soldier.
    2 a kind of chocolate.
    3 a priest from Rome.
    4 a place in Italy.

(27) Why did Claudius II make a new rule?

    1 He didn't want soldiers to get married.
    2 He didn't want children to become soldiers.
    3 He wanted more families to live in Rome.
    4 He wanted more people to become priests.

(28) What did Valentinus think?

    1 The leader of Rome should be kinder to women.
    2 Men and women should have families.
    3 Priests shouldn't write letters.
    4 Soldiers shouldn't go to war.

(29) What did Claudius II decide to do?

    1 Write a letter to Valentinus.
    2 Give food to poor people.
    3 Help a young girl.
    4 Kill Valentinus.

(30) What is this story about?

    1 Some soldiers who went to war.
    2 The history of Valentine's Day.
    3 A leader of Rome who had a large family.
    4 A priest who joined the army.

4

● あなたは，外国人の友達から以下のQUESTIONをされました。
● QUESTIONについて，あなたの考えとその理由を2つ英文で書きなさい。
● 語数の目安は25語～35語です。
● 解答は，解答用紙のB面にあるライティング解答欄に書きなさい。なお，解答欄の外に書かれたものは採点されません。
● 解答がQUESTIONに対応していないと判断された場合は，0点と採点されることがあります。QUESTIONをよく読んでから答えてください。

QUESTION

Which do you like better, reading books or playing video games?

リスニング

３級リスニングテストについて

1 このテストには，第1部から第3部まであります。
　☆英文は第1部では一度だけ，第2部と第3部では二度，放送されます。
　第1部：イラストを参考にしながら対話と応答を聞き，最も適切な応答を 1, 2, 3 の中から一つ選びなさい。
　第2部：対話と質問を聞き，その答えとして最も適切なものを 1, 2, 3, 4 の中から一つ選びなさい。
　第3部：英文と質問を聞き，その答えとして最も適切なものを 1, 2, 3, 4 の中から一つ選びなさい。
2 No. 30 のあと，10 秒すると試験終了の合図がありますので，筆記用具を置いてください。

||||| 第1部 ||||||||　　◀)) ▶ MP3 ▶ アプリ ▶ CD2 **1**～**11**

〔例題〕

No. 1

No. 2

No. 3

No. 4

No. 5

No. 6

No. 7

No. 8

No. 9

No. 10

No. 11
1 One cup.
2 Two cups.
3 Five cups.
4 Six cups.

No. 12
1 At the cafeteria.
2 At her house.
3 At the French restaurant.
4 At the man's house.

No. 13
1 Sally.
2 Karen.
3 Scott.
4 Bob.

No. 14
1 Learn how to use the computer.
2 Take the boy to a restaurant.
3 Finish her homework.
4 Make dinner.

No. 15
1 This morning.
2 This afternoon.
3 Tomorrow morning.
4 Tomorrow afternoon.

No. 16
1 The tickets are very cheap.
2 The movie theater is closed.
3 They won a movie poster.
4 They saw a famous person.

No. 17	1 The boy's dog ran away.
	2 The boy bought a new pet.
	3 The boy caught a cold.
	4 The boy's dog came home.
No. 18	1 She bought a CD.
	2 She met her favorite band.
	3 She gave her friend a CD.
	4 She went to band practice.
No. 19	1 Finish his homework.
	2 Turn off the TV.
	3 Watch the soccer game.
	4 Give back her math textbook.
No. 20	1 A restaurant.
	2 A clothes shop.
	3 A hotel.
	4 A fashion magazine.

No. 21　　1 Concert tickets.
　　　　　　　2 Some CDs.
　　　　　　　3 A book.
　　　　　　　4 A card.

No. 22　　1 In New York.
　　　　　　　2 In Tokyo.
　　　　　　　3 In Seattle.
　　　　　　　4 In Toronto.

No. 23　　1 Three months ago.
　　　　　　　2 Four months ago.
　　　　　　　3 Five months ago.
　　　　　　　4 Six months ago.

No. 24　　1 To get money for his trip.
　　　　　　　2 To buy books.
　　　　　　　3 To pay for his Spanish lessons.
　　　　　　　4 To buy a new car.

No. 25　　1 His new bike.
　　　　　　　2 His new house.
　　　　　　　3 A station near a park.
　　　　　　　4 A park by his office.

No. 26　　1 For thirty minutes.
　　　　　　　2 For one hour.
　　　　　　　3 For one and a half hours.
　　　　　　　4 For two hours.

No. 27	1 A Christmas card.
	2 A wallet.
	3 Some sunglasses.
	4 Some socks.
No. 28	1 Travel to Brazil.
	2 Write a story about her father.
	3 Show her father some photos.
	4 Buy a camera.
No. 29	1 Under his car.
	2 Under the sofa.
	3 On his bed.
	4 On the table.
No. 30	1 Sunny.
	2 Rainy.
	3 Cloudy.
	4 Snowy.

A Popular Food

Tempura is a popular Japanese food. Fresh vegetables and seafood are cooked in hot oil. Many people enjoy eating tempura at restaurants, but some people like to make tempura at home.

Questions

No. 1   Please look at the passage. Where do many people enjoy eating tempura?

No. 2   Please look at the picture. What is the woman looking at?

No. 3   Please look at the man with a cap. What is he doing?

Now, Mr. / Ms. ——, please turn the card over.

No. 4   What kind of pet do you want?

No. 5   Do you like to go shopping?
                  Yes. → What do you like to buy?
                  No. → Where do you like to go with your friends?

The Winter Games

The Winter Olympic Games are an international sports event. People from many countries try hard to win a gold medal. Snowboarding and skating are exciting to watch, so they are enjoyed by many people.

Questions

No. 1   Please look at the passage. Why are snowboarding and skating enjoyed by many people?

No. 2   Please look at the picture. How many people are carrying bags?

No. 3   Please look at the man. What is he going to do?

Now, Mr. / Ms. ——, please turn the card over.

No. 4   Where do you often go on weekends?

No. 5   Do you like to go swimming?
　　　　　　Yes. → Please tell me more.
　　　　　　No. → What do you usually do with your friends?

2018-2

一次試験 2018.10.7 実施
二次試験 A日程 2018.11.4 実施
　　　　 B日程 2018.11.11 実施

Grade 3

試験時間

筆記：50分
リスニング：約25分

一次試験・筆記　　　　　p.90〜100
一次試験・リスニングp.101〜106
二次試験・面接　　　　　p.108〜111

＊解答・解説は別冊p.113〜148にあります。
＊面接の流れは本書p.9にあります。

2018年度第2回 **Web特典「自動採点サービス」対応**
オンラインマークシート
※検定の回によってQRコードが違います。
※筆記1〜3，リスニングの採点ができます。
※PCからも利用できます（本書 p.8 参照）。

1 次の (1) から (15) までの (　) に入れるのに最も適切なものを 1, 2, 3, 4 の中から一つ選び，その番号のマーク欄をぬりつぶしなさい。

(1) Steven's father makes very good pizza. He is a (　) at an Italian restaurant.

1 guide　　　**2** florist　　　**3** chef　　　**4** hairdresser

(2) *A:* Excuse me. How can I get to the hospital?
B: Go three (　) and turn left.

1 sights　　　**2** facts　　　**3** models　　　**4** blocks

(3) Mr. Brown is one of the (　) for our college English speech contest.

1 musicians　　**2** scientists　　**3** judges　　**4** doctors

(4) Last Saturday, my family (　) my grandmother's 100th birthday at a nice restaurant.

1 celebrated　　**2** clicked　　**3** carried　　**4** complained

(5) *A:* The weather was really (　) yesterday.
B: Yes, there wasn't a cloud in the sky.

1 heavy　　　**2** dark　　　**3** fine　　　**4** rainy

(6) *A:* What do you want to watch on TV?
B: There is a quiz show at 7 p.m. It's on (　) eight. Let's watch that.

1 place　　　**2** area　　　**3** side　　　**4** channel

(7) This restaurant (　) really good Chinese food.

1 reaches　　**2** serves　　**3** covers　　**4** invites

(8) *A:* Jackie looks a little sad these days.
B: Let's visit her and try to (　　　) her up.
1 leave　　　**2** let　　　**3** please　　　**4** cheer

(9) *A:* Where did you (　　　) up, David?
B: In San Francisco.
1 grow　　　**2** lose　　　**3** rise　　　**4** sound

(10) *A:* Is Fred home, Mrs. Brown?
B: No, he isn't.　But he'll be back in a (　　　) minutes.
1 small　　　**2** many　　　**3** few　　　**4** large

(11) *A:* I'm not very good at playing the piano, Dad.
B: You just have to (　　　) practicing.　You'll get better soon.
1 give　　　**2** keep　　　**3** help　　　**4** bring

(12) *A:* Paul, it's raining hard now, so I'll give you a (　　　) to the train station.
B: Thanks, Mom.
1 reason　　　**2** ride　　　**3** rain　　　**4** room

(13) Students (　　　) want to enter the speech contest have to come to the gym at lunchtime.
1 who　　　**2** what　　　**3** whose　　　**4** why

(14) Simon needs a new bike.　His old bike was (　　　).
1 steal　　　**2** stole　　　**3** stolen　　　**4** stealing

(15) *A:* Sam, I'd like you (　　　) Susan with her math homework.
B: Sure.
1 help　　　**2** helped　　　**3** be helped　　　**4** to help

次の (16) から (20) までの会話について, (   ) に入れるのに最も適切なもの
を 1, 2, 3, 4 の中から一つ選び, その番号のマーク欄をぬりつぶしなさい。

(16) *Father:* Jimmy, why is the window broken?
  Son: Sorry, Dad. (   ) Bill and I were playing catch
     in the yard.
  1 It was an accident.   **2** I enjoy watching baseball.
  3 The game starts at four.   **4** I'll get a new glove.

(17) *Salesclerk:* Good afternoon, sir. Can I help you?
  Customer: I like this coat. (   )
  Salesclerk: Sure. There is a mirror over there.
  1 Can I come back later?
  2 How many are there?
  3 Where are the men's shoes?
  4 Can I try it on?

(18) *Girl:* I've never seen this comic book before. Where did you
     get it?
  Boy: (   ) but it's sold at Ashley's Bookstore, too.
  1 You should read it,   **2** I bought it on the Internet,
  3 It was only five dollars,   **4** I left it at school,

(19) *Girl:* I really like your older sister. She's so kind.
  Boy: I know. When I'm sad, (   )
  1 she's never nice to me.
  2 I have a brother, too.
  3 she always makes me happy.
  4 I'm two years younger than her.

(20) *Woman 1:* Wow! This is a really nice apartment. (   )
  Woman 2: I moved here last summer.
  1 Where did you live before?
  2 How long have you lived here?
  3 Why is it so hot?
  4 How often do you clean it?

（筆記試験の問題は次のページに続きます。）

Come to Brownsville Church's Charity Event and Help Sick Children!

Are you looking for clothes or toys for your children? You'll find these things and much more at Brownsville Church's charity event!

Date: Saturday, November 23
Time: 10 a.m.−4 p.m.
Place: Brownsville Field, 130 Johnson Street (behind the post office)

If it rains, the event will be held in the city hall.

We need your support. We'll send all the money
from this event to a children's hospital in India.

To find out more about the event, please check our website below:
www.brownsvillechurch.org

(21) If it doesn't rain, the event will be held

    1 in the city hall.
    2 in front of the post office.
    3 behind Brownsville Church.
    4 at Brownsville Field.

(22) Why is the church having the event?

    1 To build a hospital in Brownsville.
    2 To buy clothes for children in Brownsville.
    3 To collect money for sick children in India.
    4 To send toys to a city hall in India.

From: Paul Harrison
To: Greg Harrison
Date: March 16
Subject: Spring vacation

Uncle Greg,
How are you? I'm looking forward to staying with you in Boston during my spring vacation. My mother told me to send you some information about my train schedule. She's a little worried because this is my first time to travel alone. My train arrives at South Station at 5:30 on Friday evening. I can walk to your apartment from there. I remember where you live.
I can't wait to see you!
Paul

From: Greg Harrison
To: Paul Harrison
Date: March 17
Subject: Your visit

Hi Paul,
I'm looking forward to seeing you, too. I have to work until 5:30 on Friday, so wait at the train station. There is a big café on the first floor. I'll see you there at around 5:45. After that, we'll go out for dinner at the oldest restaurant in Boston. My friend Jane is planning to come with us. Do you remember her? I'm going to take you sightseeing on Saturday afternoon. And let's go and watch a baseball game on Saturday night. I've already bought two tickets. Is there anything else you want to do? I know you like to draw pictures. How about going to the city art museum?
See you soon,
Uncle Greg

From: Paul Harrison
To: Greg Harrison
Date: March 17
Subject: Sounds good

Uncle Greg,
Of course I remember Jane. She's very nice. All of your plans sound great. I can't wait to see the baseball game. Thanks for buying the tickets. Also, I'd love to go to the art museum. I heard that it's really good. Let's go there on Sunday. I'll bring some of my pictures to show you and Jane, too.
See you on Friday evening,
Paul

(23) Why is Paul's mother worried?

    1 Paul has never traveled by himself before.
    2 The train to Boston is often late.
    3 Paul's uncle's apartment is very small.
    4 Paul hasn't been to a big city before.

(24) Where will Paul meet his uncle on Friday?

    1 At his uncle's office.
    2 At his uncle's apartment.
    3 At the oldest restaurant in Boston.
    4 At a café in the train station.

(25) What does Paul want to do on Sunday?

    1 Draw some pictures.
    2 Visit an art museum.
    3 Watch a baseball game.
    4 Go to Jane's house.

Maria Tallchief

Maria Tallchief was a famous ballerina.* She was born in 1925 on a Native American reservation.* Her father was a Native American. When Maria was a child, she enjoyed music and took piano lessons. She also liked to play outside with her sister.

When Maria was eight, her family moved to Los Angeles, California. Her mother loved music and dance. She hoped that Maria and her brothers and sisters would become movie stars. Maria soon started taking ballet classes. Every day, she practiced piano and ballet. However, when she was 12, her father told her to choose between piano and ballet. Maria chose ballet.

Maria started taking dance classes at a new ballet school. Her teacher was a famous ballerina named Madame Nijinska. Madame Nijinska was from Russia, and she taught Maria for the next five years. When Maria was 17, she moved to New York to join a famous ballet company* called the Ballet Russe de Monte Carlo.

While Maria was a dancer with the Ballet Russe de Monte Carlo, she met a famous choreographer* named George Balanchine. Balanchine liked Maria's dancing, so he often gave her important parts in his ballet performances. Maria traveled around the world and danced in many countries. Later, Maria and Balanchine got married, and Balanchine left the Ballet Russe de Monte Carlo. He started his own ballet company called the New York City Ballet. Maria soon joined the company and became its star ballerina. Later, she became a ballet teacher and worked for some famous ballet companies.

*ballerina：バレリーナ
*Native American reservation：アメリカ先住民の保留地
*company：集団
*choreographer：振付師

(26) When Maria Tallchief was a child, she

   1 liked music and playing outside.
   2 performed in a play at school.
   3 was a famous pianist.
   4 met a famous movie star.

(27) How old was Maria when she moved to California?

   1 Five.
   2 Eight.
   3 Twelve.
   4 Seventeen.

(28) Why did Maria go to New York?

   1 She wanted to join a famous ballet company.
   2 She didn't like Madame Nijinska.
   3 She wanted to live with her brothers and sisters.
   4 She was told to go there by her father.

(29) What did George Balanchine do for Maria?

   1 He gave her important parts in his ballet performances.
   2 He introduced her to a star ballerina.
   3 He sent her presents from many countries.
   4 He took her to see the New York City Ballet.

(30) What is this story about?

   1 A ballet company from Russia.
   2 A popular piano teacher from New York.
   3 A famous Native American ballerina.
   4 A big dance school in the United States.

4

- あなたは，外国人の友達から以下のQUESTIONをされました。
- QUESTIONについて，あなたの考えとその理由を2つ英文で書きなさい。
- 語数の目安は25語～35語です。
- 解答は，解答用紙のB面にあるライティング解答欄に書きなさい。なお，解答欄の外に書かれたものは採点されません。
- 解答がQUESTIONに対応していないと判断された場合は，0点と採点されることがあります。QUESTIONをよく読んでから答えてください。

QUESTION

Which do you like better, nature or big cities?

リスニング

３級リスニングテストについて

1 このテストには，第1部から第3部まであります。
   ☆英文は第1部では一度だけ，第2部と第3部では二度，放送されます。
   第1部：イラストを参考にしながら対話と応答を聞き，最も適切な応答を 1, 2, 3 の中から一つ選びなさい。
   第2部：対話と質問を聞き，その答えとして最も適切なものを 1, 2, 3, 4 の中から一つ選びなさい。
   第3部：英文と質問を聞き，その答えとして最も適切なものを 1, 2, 3, 4 の中から一つ選びなさい。
2 No. 30 のあと，10 秒すると試験終了の合図がありますので，筆記用具を置いてください。

||||| 第1部 ||||| 🔊 ▶MP3 ▶アプリ ▶CD 2 **43**～**53**

〔例題〕

No. 1

No. 2

No. 3

No. 4

No. 5

No. 6

No. 7

No. 8

No. 9

No. 10

No. 11
1 Call the dentist.
2 See a movie.
3 Stay at home.
4 Buy some candy.

No. 12
1 Go to work.
2 Make dinner.
3 Wash the dishes.
4 Eat at a restaurant.

No. 13
1 $3.
2 $5.
3 $10.
4 $20.

No. 14
1 Hers.
2 Her father's.
3 Her aunt's.
4 Her friend's.

No. 15
1 She is sick.
2 She has already eaten.
3 She doesn't have enough money.
4 She has to work.

No. 16
1 On March 7.
2 On March 12.
3 On March 18.
4 On March 20.

No. 17	1 Go shopping.
	2 Visit her cousin.
	3 Watch TV.
	4 Play badminton.
No. 18	1 Six.
	2 Nine.
	3 Ten.
	4 Fifteen.
No. 19	1 The science room.
	2 Their new teacher.
	3 A science test.
	4 A new club.
No. 20	1 At 3:00.
	2 At 5:00.
	3 At 5:30.
	4 At 7:00.

No. 21
1 On a bus.
2 On a plane.
3 On a train.
4 On a boat.

No. 22
1 Her favorite teacher.
2 Her friend from school.
3 Her uncle.
4 Her parents.

No. 23
1 Visiting France.
2 Talking to her French teacher.
3 Getting a letter from France.
4 Meeting some French students.

No. 24
1 For one hour.
2 For two hours.
3 For four hours.
4 For five hours.

No. 25
1 He didn't eat lunch.
2 He woke up late.
3 The supermarket moved.
4 The supermarket was closed.

No. 26
1 She hurt her leg.
2 Her train was late.
3 She missed her train.
4 The station was crowded.

18年度第2回　リスニング

No. 27	1 He is a good artist.
	2 He works in a museum.
	3 He teaches art every day.
	4 He buys many paintings.
No. 28	1 Rainy.
	2 Snowy.
	3 Sunny.
	4 Stormy.
No. 29	1 A cat.
	2 A dog.
	3 A mouse.
	4 A rabbit.
No. 30	1 He listened to his favorite band.
	2 He sang a song to his son.
	3 He took his son to school.
	4 He made breakfast.

面　接

Coffee Shops

There are coffee shops everywhere in Japan.　Coffee shops sell many kinds of cakes and drinks, so they are good places to relax with friends.　Some people also like to read books there.

Questions

No. 1   Please look at the passage. Why are coffee shops good places to relax with friends?

No. 2   Please look at the picture. Where is the magazine?

No. 3   Please look at the woman with long hair. What is she going to do?

Now, Mr. / Ms. ——, please turn the card over.

No. 4   Where would you like to go on your next holiday?

No. 5   Have you ever been to an aquarium?

        Yes. → Please tell me more.

        No. → What do you like to do in the evenings?

18年度第2回 面接

Fishing

There are many rivers and lakes in Japan. On weekends, many people go to these places to fish. Some people don't have time to go on fishing trips, so they go to local fishing ponds.

Questions

No. 1   Please look at the passage. Why do some people go to local fishing ponds?

No. 2   Please look at the picture. How many men are fishing?

No. 3   Please look at the girl. What is she doing?

Now, Mr. / Ms. ——, please turn the card over.

No. 4   What did you do last night?

No. 5   Have you ever been snowboarding?
           Yes. → Please tell me more.
           No. → What would you like to do on your next vacation?

2018-1

一次試験　2018.6.3実施
二次試験　A日程　2018.7.1実施
　　　　　B日程　2018.7.8実施

Grade 3

試験時間

筆記：**50分**
リスニング：約**25分**

＊解答・解説は別冊p.149〜184にあります。
＊面接の流れは本書p.9にあります。

2018年度第1回　**Web特典「自動採点サービス」対応
オンラインマークシート**
※検定の回によってQRコードが違います。
※筆記1〜3，リスニングの採点ができます。
※ PC からも利用できます（本書 p.8 参照）。

1 次の (1) から (15) までの (　　) に入れるのに最も適切なものを **1, 2, 3, 4** の中から一つ選び, その番号のマーク欄をぬりつぶしなさい。

(1) **A:** Before you (　　　　) the street, always look left and right to check for cars.
B: Yes, Dad.
1 break　　　　**2** cross　　　　**3** put　　　　**4** lend

(2) When I went to the restaurant, it was closed. A (　　　　) on the door said it would open again tomorrow.
1 couple　　**2** hill　　**3** sign　　**4** goal

(3) **A:** Did you hear about Tony's skiing (　　　　)?
B: Yes. He has a broken leg.
1 type　　　　　　　　　　**2** accident
3 environment　　　　　　**4** horizon

(4) **A:** Last Saturday, my cousins came to visit. We had a big dinner and enjoyed talking with each other.
B: That (　　　) like fun.
1 sounds　　**2** cries　　**3** feels　　**4** plans

(5) After the new airport opened, more (　　　) started to visit the island to enjoy the beautiful beaches and warm weather.
1 assistants　　**2** scientists　　**3** winners　　**4** tourists

(6) Tom likes books. The (　　　) of his favorite book is *Robinson Crusoe*.
1 title　　**2** prize　　**3** middle　　**4** hole

(7) **A:** I don't know much about baseball. Can you (　　　) the rules to me?
B: Sure. It's easy.
1 sell　　**2** save　　**3** happen　　**4** explain

(8) We had our first English lesson today. Our teacher, Mr. Brown, ( ) himself and told us about his hobbies.

1 believed   **2** asked   **3** clicked   **4** introduced

(9) I got this T-shirt for my birthday. At ( ), I didn't like the color very much, but now it's my favorite. I wear it all the time.

1 first   **2** front   **3** once   **4** then

(10) *A:* This jacket is a little big for me. Can I ( ) on a smaller one?

B: Certainly, sir. How about this one?

1 hit   **2** make   **3** enter   **4** try

(11) *A:* Bob, could you give me a ( )? I have to move this desk.

B: Sure.

1 face   **2** hand   **3** finger   **4** head

(12) *A:* What did you buy for your brother, Nancy?

B: I bought him a ( ) of jogging shoes.

1 piece   **2** space   **3** pair   **4** time

(13) *A:* When ( ) your violin lesson start, Nancy?

B: At five, Dad.

1 is   **2** are   **3** do   **4** does

(14) My little brother lost my favorite CD again. He really makes ( ) angry.

1 me   **2** my   **3** we   **4** our

(15) *A:* Jane, do you know ( ) Mary went home early today?

B: Yes. She is sick.

1 whose   **2** which   **3** where   **4** why

(16)   *Man:* I'm going for lunch now.
        Woman: Me, too. I'm going to get a sandwich. (   )
        Man: I feel like eating noodles.
        1 What about you?   2 What do we have?
        3 Why do you think so?   4 Why are you here?

(17) *Girl 1:* Can your sister come to the beach tomorrow?
      Girl 2: (   ) If she can come, maybe she can drive us.
      1 I'll be there soon.
      2 I bought a new swimsuit.
      3 I got chairs for us.
      4 I'll ask her tonight.

(18) *Boy:* How's your science project going?
      Girl: (   ) I'm going to do it this weekend.
      1 It was during math class.
      2 I went on Saturday.
      3 I haven't started yet.
      4 It's not my idea.

(19) *Husband:* We should leave soon. (   )
          Wife: Almost. I'm just looking for my bag.
      Husband: It's here, by the kitchen table.
      1 Will you buy one?   2 Are you ready?
      3 Can you make lunch?   4 Shall we go by taxi?

(20) *Boy 1:* Do you usually have tennis practice on Wednesdays?
      Boy 2: No, but (   ) I need to practice hard for my big
          game on Saturday.
      1 I do this week.
      2 my sister won.
      3 you're a great player.
      4 this is my favorite racket.

（筆記試験の問題は次のページに続きます。）

Summer Camp

When: June 23 to June 25
Cost: $250 (Please pay on June 10.)

This June, seventh-grade students can go camping at Cider Lake. You can swim in the lake, go hiking, and more! There will be a barbecue on the last night. It'll be cold, so bring warm clothes.

The bus will leave at 9 a.m. on June 23. We'll arrive at the camp before noon and eat there. You don't have to bring lunch.

If you want to come, sign up in the teachers' room by June 2. You must also come to the meeting in the library at 4 p.m. on June 10.

(21) What do students need to take to the camp?

    1 Warm clothes.
    2 Lunch for the first day.
    3 Some money.
    4 Food for the barbecue.

(22) Students who will go to the camp must

    1 be able to swim well.
    2 pay $250 before June 2.
    3 go to the meeting on June 10.
    4 go to the teachers' room on June 23.

次のEメールの内容に関して, (23) から (25) までの質問に対する答えとして最も適切なものを 1, 2, 3, 4 の中から一つ選び, その番号のマーク欄をぬりつぶしなさい。

From: Sarah Blake
To: Jane Robinson
Date: July 23
Subject: Dance class

Dear Ms. Robinson,
I saw a poster about hip-hop dance classes at your dance school when I went to Toronto City Hall yesterday. Are there any classes for junior high school students on Saturday mornings or afternoons? I can't take lessons on weekdays because I usually have tennis practice after school. Also, I'd like to know how many students are in the classes. And do your students sometimes perform at events? I have never taken dance lessons before.
Best regards,
Sarah

From: Jane Robinson
To: Sarah Blake
Date: July 24
Subject: Free lesson

Dear Sarah,
Thank you for your e-mail. We have two hip-hop dance classes for junior high school students. One is on Saturdays from 10 a.m., and the other is on Sundays from 2 p.m. The Saturday class has nine students. The Sunday one just started, so it's still small. It only has four students, but we hope another five or six will join soon. Every summer, all of our students perform at the Toronto Summer Festival. It's a big event, so they practice very hard. Can you come this Saturday or Sunday for a free lesson? If you enjoy the lesson, you can join the class. Please bring a towel and wear comfortable shoes and clothes. Let me know if you can come.

Sincerely,
Jane Robinson

From: Sarah Blake
To: Jane Robinson
Date: July 24
Subject: Thank you

Dear Ms. Robinson,
Thank you very much for the information about the hip-hop dance classes. I'd like to take a free lesson on Saturday. If it's OK, my mother will come and watch. I'm really excited about it!
See you soon,
Sarah

(23) Where did Sarah see the poster about hip-hop dance classes?

    1 At the city hall.
    2 At Jane Robinson's house.
    3 At the tennis court.
    4 At her junior high school.

(24) How many students are in the Sunday afternoon class now?

    1 Four.
    2 Five.
    3 Six.
    4 Nine.

(25) What did Sarah decide to do?

    1 Join the Sunday class.
    2 Go to the Toronto Summer Festival.
    3 Watch her mother's dance lesson.
    4 Try a free lesson on Saturday.

次の英文の内容に関して，(26) から (30) までの質問に対する答えとして最も適切なもの，または文を完成させるのに最も適切なものを 1, 2, 3, 4 の中から一つ選び，その番号のマーク欄をぬりつぶしなさい。

Snacks for Sailors*

Crackers are a popular snack all over the world. There are many different shapes and flavors of crackers. Some people like to eat them with cheese or meat on them, and others eat them without anything. Saltines are a very popular kind of cracker. They are square crackers with salt on them, and they also have many small holes.

Crackers were invented in 1792 by John Pearson in Massachusetts in the United States. Pearson owned a bakery, and he wanted to make a kind of food for sailors. Sailors often took bread with them on ships, but the bread spoiled* quickly. Pearson mixed flour and water together, and he baked it until it was very dry. He named his new food Pearson's Pilot Bread, but many sailors called it "hardtack."

The English word "cracker" was not used until 1801. At that time, a man named Josiah Bent had his own hardtack bakery. One day, Bent was baking pieces of hardtack. The pieces burned, and they made a crackling sound.* When he heard this sound, he thought of the word "cracker." Bent also wanted to sell his crackers to people other than sailors. He put salt in his recipe to make them more delicious.

Bent's crackers became very popular in the northeastern United States, and people there often put them in soup. Soon, people in other parts of the country began eating them. Later, a company called Nabisco bought both Pearson's and Bent's bakeries. Nabisco continued to use Bent's recipe, but it gave the crackers a new name, saltines.

*sailor：船員
*spoil：腐る
*crackling sound：パチパチする音

122

(26) Saltines are crackers that

    1 have small holes in them.
    2 have many different shapes.
    3 are made from cheese.
    4 are often cooked with meat.

(27) Why did John Pearson make Pearson's Pilot Bread?

    1 He couldn't find good food in Massachusetts.
    2 He could buy flour and water very cheaply.
    3 He didn't like dry food.
    4 He wanted to make a kind of food for sailors.

(28) Why did Josiah Bent put salt in his recipe for crackers?

    1 To make them easier to bake.
    2 To make them more delicious.
    3 To burn them more quickly.
    4 To get more sailors to buy them.

(29) What did the company called Nabisco do?

    1 It bought two bakeries.
    2 It built a new ship for sailors.
    3 It made a special soup for crackers.
    4 It opened many restaurants in the United States.

(30) What is this story about?

    1 The history of an English word.
    2 The history of a famous company.
    3 The history of a popular snack.
    4 The history of food on ships.

4

● あなたは，外国人の友達から以下のQUESTIONをされました。

● QUESTIONについて，あなたの考えとその理由を2つ英文で書きなさい。

● 語数の目安は25語〜35語です。

● 解答は，解答用紙のB面にあるライティング解答欄に書きなさい。なお，解答欄の外に書かれたものは採点されません。

● 解答がQUESTIONに対応していないと判断された場合は，0点と採点されることがあります。QUESTIONをよく読んでから答えてください。

QUESTION

Which do you like better, talking with your friends or talking with your family?

リスニング

３級リスニングテストについて

1 このテストには，第1部から第3部まであります。
 ☆英文は第1部では一度だけ，第2部と第3部では二度，放送されます。
 第1部：イラストを参考にしながら対話と応答を聞き，最も適切な応答を 1, 2, 3 の中から一つ選びなさい。
 第2部：対話と質問を聞き，その答えとして最も適切なものを 1, 2, 3, 4 の中から一つ選びなさい。
 第3部：英文と質問を聞き，その答えとして最も適切なものを 1, 2, 3, 4 の中から一つ選びなさい。
2 No. 30 のあと，10 秒すると試験終了の合図がありますので，筆記用具を置いてください。

‖‖‖ 第1部 ‖‖‖ 🔊 ▶MP3 ▶アプリ ▶CD3 **1**〜**11**

〔例題〕

No. 1

No. 2

125

No. 3

No. 4

No. 5

No. 6

No. 7

No. 8

No. 9

No. 10

No. 11
1 Sunny.
2 Snowy.
3 Hot.
4 Rainy.

No. 12
1 Tonight.
2 Tomorrow morning.
3 Tomorrow afternoon.
4 Next week.

No. 13
1 On her desk.
2 On the floor.
3 In her bag.
4 In the school office.

No. 14
1 Write a letter to his friend.
2 Go to the girl's house.
3 Study for a test.
4 Start writing a report.

No. 15
1 Go out to play.
2 Cook his dinner.
3 Help his mother.
4 Eat some dessert.

No. 16
1 Go to the bus station.
2 Wait for the train.
3 Take a taxi.
4 Buy another ticket.

No. 17	1 He doesn't like the color.
	2 It's too expensive.
	3 He forgot his wallet.
	4 It's not warm enough.
No. 18	1 Their lunch plans.
	2 Their trip to China.
	3 A new staff member.
	4 The woman's part-time job.
No. 19	1 The girl's mother.
	2 The girl's father.
	3 The boy.
	4 The boy's father.
No. 20	1 Once.
	2 Twice.
	3 Three times.
	4 Four times.

No. 21
1 Tim won a writing contest.
2 Tim went to Brazil.
3 Tim went on a school trip.
4 Tim's story was in a newspaper.

No. 22
1 Before dinner tonight.
2 After dinner tonight.
3 Before lunch on Saturday.
4 After lunch on Saturday.

No. 23
1 For two weeks.
2 For three weeks.
3 For two months.
4 For three months.

No. 24
1 He watched a movie.
2 He ate at a restaurant.
3 He bought a ticket to a game.
4 He met his favorite player.

No. 25
1 At an airport.
2 At a hospital.
3 In a cafeteria.
4 In a museum.

No. 26
1 Visit a farm.
2 Buy a new bike.
3 Borrow some books.
4 Go to a zoo.

No. 27	1 Make breakfast.
	2 Buy a birthday cake.
	3 Study French.
	4 Take cooking lessons.

No. 28	1 The tennis club.
	2 The table tennis club.
	3 The soccer club.
	4 The volleyball club.

No. 29	1 He was angry with Sarah.
	2 He had to go to work.
	3 He didn't know anyone there.
	4 He wasn't feeling well.

No. 30	1 He can't find a job.
	2 He lost his house kcy.
	3 He doesn't enjoy his job.
	4 He lives far from his office.

Eating Fish

In Japan, many people enjoy eating fish. Fish tastes good when it is fresh, so it is sold at markets early in the morning. Eating fish can be very good for your health.

Questions

No. 1   Please look at the passage. Why is fish sold at markets early in the morning?

No. 2   Please look at the picture. What is the man with glasses carrying?

No. 3   Please look at the woman. What is she going to do?

Now, Mr. / Ms. ——, please turn the card over.

No. 4   What do you usually do after dinner?

No. 5   Have you ever been on a plane?
           Yes. → Please tell me more.
           No. → What did you do last Sunday?

The Rainy Season

In Japan, it often rains in June and July. Some gardens look beautiful when it rains, so they are nice places to visit during the rainy season. This season is also important for growing rice.

Questions

No. 1   Please look at the passage. Why are some gardens nice places to visit during the rainy season?

No. 2   Please look at the picture. How many people are holding umbrellas?

No. 3   Please look at the girls on the stage. What are they doing?

Now, Mr. / Ms. ——, please turn the card over.

No. 4   What kind of pet do you want?

No. 5   Are you good at playing sports?
            Yes. → Please tell me more.
            No. → What do you like to do when you are at home?

2017-3

一次試験 2018.1.21実施
二次試験 A日程 2018.2.18実施
　　　　 B日程 2018.2.25実施

Grade 3

試験時間

筆記：50分
リスニング：約25分

＊解答・解説は別冊p.185～220にあります。
＊面接の流れは本書p.9にあります。

2017年度第3回

Web特典「自動採点サービス」対応
オンラインマークシート
※検定の回によってQRコードが違います。
※筆記1～3，リスニングの採点ができます。
※ PC からも利用できます（本書 p.8 参照）。

1 次の **(1)** から **(15)** までの (　　) に入れるのに最も適切なものを **1, 2, 3, 4** の中から一つ選び，その番号のマーク欄をぬりつぶしなさい。

(1) Come and watch the baseball game on TV, Dad. Your favorite team is (　　).
1 winning **2** selling **3** belonging **4** filling

(2) Keiko's family lives in an apartment now, but they are going to (　　) a new house next year.
1 taste **2** imagine **3** invite **4** build

(3) *A:* What do you want to be when you grow up?
B: I'm not sure. I don't have any plans for my (　　) yet.
1 shape **2** future **3** energy **4** culture

(4) My brother is going to (　　) to Nagoya next month because he's starting a new job there.
1 move **2** smile **3** hear **4** wait

(5) *A:* Excuse me. Is the post office near here?
B: It's just over there, on the other (　　) of the street.
1 line **2** side **3** way **4** source

(6) *A:* How was your weekend, Mr. Brown?
B: Very nice. I (　　) most of the weekend reading books.
1 gave **2** bought **3** made **4** spent

(7) *A:* What should I (　　) to the party tonight, Nancy?
B: A jacket and a tie.
1 invent **2** set **3** wear **4** put

(8) The TV star spoke too fast. Fred couldn't understand her at
( ).

1 ever   **2** all   **3** much   **4** never

(9) *A:* Do you have any pets, John?
B: No, I'm afraid ( ) cats and dogs.

1 at   **2** on   **3** for   **4** of

(10) *A:* I didn't see you at school yesterday.
B: I was ( ) in bed all day with a cold. But I'm feeling better now.

1 sick   **2** after   **3** up   **4** silent

(11) *A:* The music is too loud. Please ( ) down the radio.
B: All right.

1 go   **2** make   **3** stand   **4** turn

(12) Mary's dog ran ( ) yesterday because she forgot to close the gate.

1 with   **2** away   **3** from   **4** above

(13) My sister loves music. She is good at ( ).

1 sing   **2** sings   **3** sang   **4** singing

(14) *A:* Charles will meet us at the airport tomorrow, ( ) he?
B: I think so.

1 doesn't   **2** can't   **3** isn't   **4** won't

(15) *A:* Who is that man ( ) on the bench over there?
B: That's my father.

1 sit   **2** sat   **3** sitting   **4** sits

2 次の (16) から (20) までの会話について，( ) に入れるのに最も適切なものを 1, 2, 3, 4 の中から一つ選び，その番号のマーク欄をぬりつぶしなさい。

(16) **Boy:** I'm sorry, Tina. I forgot to bring your dictionary to school.
Girl: That's OK. ( )
1 It's not on my desk.   2 It's in my locker.
3 I'm using it now.   4 I don't need it today.

(17)   **Grandson:** Could I have some more pie?
Grandmother: Sure. Here you are. ( )
    Grandson: Yes, thanks.
1 Is that enough?   2 Did you buy some apples?
3 Are they open?   4 Do you often make cookies?

(18) **Girl:** I'm so nervous about tomorrow's Spanish test.
Boy: ( ) You'll pass easily.
1 I'll ask the teacher.   2 Don't worry about it.
3 Thanks for that.   4 I've never been there.

(19)   **Wife:** I was looking for the pictures from your sister's wedding, but I couldn't find them.
Husband: ( ) I'll go and get them for you.
1 I'll buy the tickets tomorrow.
2 You can use my camera.
3 We went by plane.
4 They're in a box upstairs.

(20) **Boy:** Tomoko, can you tell me about life in Japan?
Girl: Sure. ( )
Boy: I want to learn about the food and the people.
1 What would you like to know?
2 How long are you going to stay?
3 When did you start studying?
4 What did you enjoy the most?

（筆記試験の問題は次のページに続きます。）

次の掲示の内容に関して，(21) と (22) の質問に対する答えとして最も適切なものを 1, 2, 3, 4 の中から一つ選び，その番号のマーク欄をぬりつぶしなさい。

Important Notice from James Street Station

Special Year-End Train Schedule

Here are the changes for the year-end train schedule:

	First train	Last train	Schedule
Blue Line:	5:45 a.m.	11:45 p.m.	Trains run every 15 minutes.
Green Line:	5:50 a.m.	11:30 p.m.	Trains run every 20 minutes.

This schedule will begin on **December 30** and end on **January 1**.

Also, on January 1, exits B and C will be closed from 5:30 a.m. to noon because of the New Year's Day Parade on James Street. Every year, James Street gets very crowded, so be careful! Please see the station map or visit our website to find other exits.

www.james-st/citytrains.org

(21) What is this notice about?

    1 Making a new exit at James Street Station.
    2 Changes to the year-end train schedule.
    3 The starting time of the New Year's Day Parade.
    4 A new shop opening on James Street.

(22) What time is the first Green Line train on December 30?

    1 At 5:15 a.m.
    2 At 5:30 a.m.
    3 At 5:45 a.m.
    4 At 5:50 a.m.

次のEメールの内容に関して，(23) から (25) までの質問に対する答えとして最も適切なものを 1, 2, 3, 4 の中から一つ選び，その番号のマーク欄をぬりつぶしなさい。

From: Harry Yates
To: Barbara Yates
Date: July 18
Subject: I can't wait!

Dear Aunt Barbara,
How are you? Mom said you're coming to visit next month for one week. I can't wait to see you! We got a new cat last month, and her name is Pepper. We named her that because she's black and gray. I think you'll like her. She loves to play, and she's very cute. While you're here, could you please help me with one thing? I have to give a speech in Japanese in front of my whole school in September. I'm so nervous. I've started writing my speech, but it's really difficult. Could you help me with it? Mom says you studied Japanese when you were at college, so I'm sure you're very good.
See you soon,
Harry

From: Barbara Yates
To: Harry Yates
Date: July 19
Subject: Sure!

Hi Harry,
I'm looking forward to seeing you next month, too. And I'd love to help you with your Japanese speech. Let's do some other things while I'm visiting, too. How about going to the science museum in Grand City? One of my friends has a part-time job there. If she's not busy, she'll be able to give us a special tour. Also, I can't wait to meet Pepper. She sounds lovely. Your mom and I had a cat when we were kids, too. His name was Tiger, but he wasn't orange and black. He was white. He looked like a white tiger that your

mom saw at the zoo, so she thought Tiger was a good name for him.

See you next month,

Barbara

(23) What does Harry ask his aunt to do?

    1 Help him with his Japanese speech.

    2 Choose a name for his new pet.

    3 Look after his cat for one week.

    4 Tell him about her college life.

(24) Who works at the science museum?

    1 Harry.

    2 Harry's mother.

    3 Harry's aunt.

    4 Harry's aunt's friend.

(25) Why did Harry's mother name her cat Tiger?

    1 He looked like a white tiger.

    2 She found him outside the zoo.

    3 He was orange and black.

    4 He loved to play.

Sally Ride

Sally Ride was the first American woman to go into space. She was born in California in 1951. When she was growing up, she loved math, science, and tennis. In high school, she became a very good tennis player. In fact, she was one of the best players in America. At that time, she wanted to become a professional tennis player. She practiced hard every day for months, but then she changed her mind. She decided to go to college instead.

Sally went to Stanford University. There, she studied science and English. Later, she got a Ph.D.* in astrophysics.* Then, in 1977, she read an advertisement* in the newspaper. It said NASA* was looking for people who wanted to become astronauts. Sally wanted the job, and she got it. She went to the Johnson Space Center in Houston, Texas, and trained to become an astronaut.

In 1983, Sally was able to go into space. Russia sent women into space in 1963 and 1982, but Sally was the first American woman to go. Her second and final trip to space was in 1984. She worked for NASA for several more years, and then she worked at Stanford University. Later, she had her own company called Sally Ride Science, and she also wrote several books.

Sadly, Sally died in 2012. However, many people remember the important things she did. In fact, in 2013, President Barack Obama gave her a special award. Also, two elementary schools are named after her. Sally is still a hero for many people.

*Ph.D.：博士号
*astrophysics：天体物理学
*advertisement：広告
*NASA：米国航空宇宙局

146

(26) What did Sally Ride want to be when she was in high school?

1 A scientist.
2 A college teacher.
3 A tennis player.
4 An astronaut.

(27) How did Sally find out about the job at NASA?

1 She read about it in the newspaper.
2 She got a call from the Johnson Space Center.
3 Her friend in Houston told her about it.
4 She saw a poster at Stanford University.

(28) How many times did Sally go to space?

1 Once.
2 Twice.
3 Three times.
4 Four times.

(29) What did President Barack Obama do in 2013?

1 He wrote a book about Sally's life.
2 He named a school after Sally.
3 He started the company Sally Ride Science.
4 He gave Sally a special award.

(30) What is this story about?

1 An important American astronaut.
2 The first woman to become the president.
3 A famous American tennis player.
4 A popular teacher who visited Russia.

4

- あなたは，外国人の友達から以下のQUESTIONをされました。
- QUESTIONについて，あなたの考えとその<u>理由を2つ</u>英文で書きなさい。
- 語数の目安は25語〜35語です。
- 解答は，解答用紙のB面にあるライティング解答欄に書きなさい。なお，<u>解答欄の外に書かれたものは採点されません。</u>
- 解答がQUESTIONに対応していないと判断された場合は，<u>0点と採点されること</u>があります。QUESTIONをよく読んでから答えてください。

QUESTION

What city do you want to visit?

リスニング

３級リスニングテストについて

1 このテストには，第1部から第3部まであります。
  ☆英文は第1部では一度だけ，第2部と第3部では二度，放送されます。
  第1部：イラストを参考にしながら対話と応答を聞き，最も適切な応答を 1, 2, 3 の中から一つ選びなさい。
  第2部：対話と質問を聞き，その答えとして最も適切なものを 1, 2, 3, 4 の中から一つ選びなさい。
  第3部：英文と質問を聞き，その答えとして最も適切なものを 1, 2, 3, 4 の中から一つ選びなさい。
2 No. 30 のあと，10 秒すると試験終了の合図がありますので，筆記用具を置いてください。

第1部   🔊 ▶MP3 ▶アプリ ▶CD 3 43〜53

〔例題〕

No. 1

No. 2

No. 3

No. 4

No. 5

No. 6

No. 7

No. 8

No. 9

No. 10

No. 11

1 Tomorrow night.
2 Next month.
3 In June.
4 In July.

No. 12

1 $1.75.
2 $2.50.
3 $3.75.
4 $5.50.

No. 13

1 Buy a new TV.
2 Move the table.
3 Watch a movie.
4 Find her friend's house.

No. 14

1 The weather was bad.
2 He was too busy.
3 He was not well.
4 He had to meet Mary.

No. 15

1 A salad made by Gina.
2 An Italian restaurant.
3 David's cooking.
4 David's garden.

No. 16

1 In his bedroom.
2 At Helen's house.
3 In the science room.
4 At the library.

17 年度第3回 リスニング

151

No. 17
1 She saw a doctor.
2 She went to a wedding.
3 She took care of her brother.
4 She called her parents.

No. 18
1 Stay home and study.
2 Take a test.
3 Meet his friend by the river.
4 Help his mother.

No. 19
1 The boy's.
2 The boy's mother's.
3 The boy's father's.
4 The boy's sister's.

No. 20
1 Eat a snack.
2 Buy some potatoes.
3 Go to a restaurant.
4 Make dinner.

No. 21
1 Yesterday morning.
2 Yesterday afternoon.
3 This morning.
4 This afternoon.

No. 22
1 His class at school.
2 His friend's family.
3 His new house.
4 His family.

No. 23
1 A school's newspaper.
2 A school's art festival.
3 A famous city.
4 A famous artist.

No. 24
1 Once.
2 Twice.
3 Three times.
4 Four times.

No. 25
1 The girl.
2 The girl's mother.
3 The girl's brother.
4 The girl's friend.

No. 26
1 He lost his notebook.
2 He forgets people's names.
3 His notebook is too small.
4 He is not good at writing.

No. 27

1 Talking with a taxi driver.
2 Making French food.
3 Teaching English.
4 Driving her new car.

No. 28

1 A new student will join the class.
2 There will be a Japanese test.
3 The teacher will be late.
4 The students will go to Japan.

No. 29

1 In her classroom.
2 In her bag.
3 In her brother's room.
4 In her brother's bag.

No. 30

1 He bought a new car.
2 He found his car keys.
3 He passed a math test.
4 He got his driver's license.

問題カード（A 日程）　　　🔊 ▶MP3 ▶アプリ ▶CD3 76〜80

Saturdays

On Saturdays, people often have some free time.　Many people go out and spend time with their friends on Saturdays, but some people like to stay home and relax.　Saturdays can be fun.

Questions

No. 1   Please look at the passage. What do many people do on Saturdays?

No. 2   Please look at the picture. Where are the flowers?

No. 3   Please look at the woman. What is she doing?

Now, Mr. / Ms. ——, please turn the card over.

No. 4   How many hours do you usually sleep every night?

No. 5   Do you like to cook?
        Yes. → Please tell me more.
        No. → Where would you like to go on your summer vacation?

Enjoying Japan

Traveling by train is a good way to see Japan. Many foreign visitors buy special train tickets, so they can travel to different places during their vacations. They can also enjoy eating delicious local food.

Questions

No. 1   Please look at the passage. Why can many foreign visitors travel to different places during their vacations?

No. 2   Please look at the picture. How many suitcases does the man have?

No. 3   Please look at the woman with long hair. What is she doing?

Now, Mr. / Ms. ——, please turn the card over.

No. 4   What do you usually have for breakfast?

No. 5   Have you ever been snowboarding?
        Yes. → Please tell me more.
        No. → What would you like to do on your next vacation?

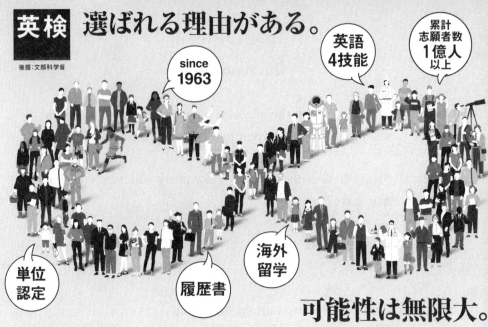
〔2020年度版 英検3級 過去6回全問題集〕　　　　　　　　　　　　　　　　S9n069